the  guide to

INTERNATIONAL DEVELOPMENT

Maggie Black

🖐 S0-BDO-968

'Publishers have created lists of short books that discuss the questions that your average [electoral] candidate will only ever touch if armed with a slogan and a soundbite. Together [such books] hint at a resurgence of the grand educational tradition... Closest to the hot headline issues are *The No-Nonsense Guides*. These target those topics that a large army of voters care about, but that politicos evade. Arguments, figures and documents combine to prove that good journalism is far too important to be left to (most) journalists.'

Boyd Tonkin,
The Independent,
London

The No-Nonsense Guide to International Development
First published in the UK by
New Internationalist™ Publications Ltd
Oxford OX4 1BW, UK
www.newint.org
New Internationalist is a registered trade mark.

in association with
Verso
6 Meard Street
London
W1V 3HR
www.versobooks.com

Cover photo: Workers in Guwahati, eastern India, demolish an illegal tall building located in an earthquake zone. Ritu Raj Konwar/AP Photo.

Design by New Internationalist Publications Ltd.
Series editor: Troth Wells

Printed by T J International Ltd, Padstow, Cornwall, UK.

British Library Cataloguing-in-Publication Data.
A catalogue record for this book is available from the British Library.

Library of Congress Cataloguing-in-Publication Data.
A catalogue for this book is available from the Library of Congress.

ISBN - 1 85984 431 6

the  NO-NONSENSE guide to

INTERNATIONAL DEVELOPMENT

Maggie Black

VERSO

About the author

Maggie Black is an independent writer and editor on social issues relating to international development, particularly in the fields of children's and women's rights, and water resources management. Among her books are: *Children first: The story of UNICEF* (OUP and UNICEF, 1996), and *A cause for our times: OXFAM, the first 50 years* (OUP and OXFAM, 1992). Other publications include: *From handpumps to health: case studies of going to scale in water and sanitation* (UNICEF, 1991); *Women and children: A development priority* (UNICEF, 1993); *Children in conflict: a child rights emergency* (UK Committee for UNICEF, 1998); *Learning what works: A 20-Year Retrospective View on International Water and Sanitation Cooperation* (World Bank/UNDP, 1998); *Child domestic work* (ICRC/UNICEF, 1999). Maggie Black is widely travelled in the developing world, especially in East Africa and South-East Asia, working as a consultant for organizations such as UNICEF, HR Wallingford, WaterAid, Anti-Slavery International, IPEC/ILO, SCF and Oxfam, and is a trustee of the UK Committee for UNICEF. She has also been an Editor of the *New Internationalist* magazine, and has written for *The Guardian*, the *Economist* and the BBC World Service.

Other titles in the series

The No-Nonsense Guide to Globalization
The No-Nonsense Guide to Fair Trade
The No-Nonsense Guide to Climate Change
The No-Nonsense Guide to International Migration
The No-Nonsense Guide to Sexual Diversity
The No-Nonsense Guide to World History
The No-Nonsense Guide to Democracy
The No-Nonsense Guide to Class, Caste & Hierarchies
The No-Nonsense Guide to The Arms Trade

Foreword

ON THE BANKS of India's river Narmada, where I write this, a battle is raging between people and development. For the past 17 years, communities here have fought non-violently against the destruction that will be wrought to their homes and livelihoods by the construction of the massive Sardar Sarovar dam. This year, with the dam height newly raised and a torrential monsoon, we are almost certain to witness the tragedy we have feared for so long. Thousands of families will lose lands and livelihoods, homes and livestock, with negligible compensation.

This battle in Narmada is part of a wider war against a perverted paradigm of development which is being imposed by means of an unprincipled, unscientific, and undemocratic process. The Narmada people's movement is one of several of its kind – the Zapatistas in Mexico, indigenous communities in the Amazon and in Canada, farmers in France, India and Philippines, and fishworkers in Japan. These movements do more than symbolize the profound resistance the prevailing development model provokes. They constitute a struggle on behalf of a different conception of what development ought to be.

The injustices perpetrated in the name of 'international development' are the starting-point of this *No-Nonsense Guide.* I welcome this, for if more people understood the damage being done to people and natural systems, tragedies such as the one we face today in the Narmada Valley might be avoided. People who depend upon the natural resource base are finding that it has been unjustly acquired, stripped from them, and its natural wealth commodified to serve the interests of a consumerist élite. Lands, water and forests are harnessed for the profit and benefit of those with power to purchase and invest – nationally and globally. Local systems of government have been forced to 'adjust', in such a way as to intensify the pauperization of those who, in many societies, still represent considerable numbers – even the majority. People faced with loss of life, dignity and livelihood have no option but to fight for their survival. From the micro-level, these movements connect into a global action demanding a major transformation of what development is and ought to be about.

Maggie Black is a writer with a difference. In this *No-Nonsense Guide to International Development* she examines the idea of development from a historical perspective, looking through different economic, social and political lenses in the search for a more just and sustainable model. But she never loses the sensitivity or descriptive power so often abandoned in analytical discourse. Those committed to the defense of the downtrodden victims of injustice and exploitation will welcome a perspective on this vast subject which places their predicament at center stage. I sincerely hope that this *Guide* reaches and informs a new section of thinking people across the world. Let as many of them as possible become not merely spectators of development and its consequences, but supporters of and even participants in the new politics of transformation.

Medha Patkar
Narmada Valley People's Movement
India

the **NO-NONSENSE** guide to

INTERNATIONAL DEVELOPMENT

CONTENTS

the **NO-NONSENSE** guide to

INTERNATIONAL DEVELOPMENT

OVER THE YEARS, what I have witnessed in villages and shantytowns has brought home to me the predicaments of those that 'development' is supposed to be about. Here is an example. 'When I was a boy, the water-holes lasted all year round. Now they dry up long before the rains. When the rivers flowed, we used to go fishing. Now the fishing baskets lie unused. We walked to school through high grass. Now the cattle have nothing to eat.'

This picture of dwindling resources, shrinking livelihoods, deepening water and food insecurity is from Namibia. But it could come from many dryland areas in Africa, and from crisis-ridden corners of India, Nepal, Bolivia, Peru – too many countries to name. This is what 'development' has done for many once self-sufficient people. Yet magisterial UN reports tell us that poverty is everywhere receding: lower child mortality, fewer illiterates, smaller families. The statistics of poverty – and they are huge – sound like an unfortunate incidental. That is far from being the case.

The destruction of traditional forms of livelihood based on the natural environment amounts in certain places to a creeping form of genocide. Yet the commodification and plunder of the commons – forests, rivers, lands, soils, water – and its accompanying pauperization carries on regardless. The benefits of the modern world that might cushion people's livelihood losses or assist their transition to an economically viable substitute are frequently deployed so as to destroy them. Something is seriously wrong.

There can be no recipe for development, only many potential recipes for different contexts. Yet the development industry advances as if the opposite were true. Some kinds of gadget, medicine, or piece of kit may have wide-scale application. But true development is about people, and social beings do not function mechanistically. There is no common prescription. To be of genuine use to people, development has to grow organically, building on existing knowledge and systems, and engaging empathetically with modern ideas. Is this really so impossible?

My worst confrontation with development as destruction came in India's Narmada Valley, where huge dams are wrecking hundreds of thousands of livelihoods. This is one example of a process endlessly repeated in different forms all over the developing world. Instead of addressing the human issues involved, politicians and their allies tend to look the other way, blaming a scapegoat, even the victims themselves. And if violent displacements from large projects are a starting point, hypocrisy is a characteristic of development in many other contexts.

The range of angles I explore is limited. Other writers would emphasize different themes – globalization, trade, democracy – covered by other titles in this series. Constrictions of space still required generalizations and syntheses I regret. Development realities are hugely diverse – which, in the end, is the best cause for optimism. Whatever the difficulties they face, some people in some parts of the world will manage to chart their own way and turn their contest with development to advantage. To them, the best of luck.

Maggie Black
Oxford

1 The history of an idea

The idea of 'development' was invented in the post-Second World War world to describe the process by which 'backward' countries would 'catch up' with the industrialized world – courtesy of its assistance. Five decades and much sobering experience later, the concept has spawned an industry of thinking and practice and undergone much evolution. However, the numbers of poor people in whose name development is justified are greater than they were when it was invented, and in many cases their poverty stems directly from the havoc it has wreaked on their lives. Under these circumstances, is the concept any longer useful?

WHERE SHOULD WE go first to understand 'development'? Let us start at San Salvador Atenco, Mexico, in January 2002.

Farmers in this agricultural area close to the capital city are protesting the forced appropriation of 33 square miles of land and the displacement of hundreds of families to make way for the construction of a new international airport. They have dug ditches to prevent heavy machinery reaching the site, taken out a case against the project in the courts, and faced down riot police in central Mexico City. But the authorities press on. Compensation is minimal, and – since agriculture is in crisis – the prospects of setting up a new farm elsewhere are negligible. 'We want our land and our freedom, and the government wants us to be taxi drivers and luggage handlers', says Ezequiel Hernandez, one of the protestors.[1]

On the other side of the world, in the Himalayan foothills, activist Sunderlal Bahuguna has just given up a similar fight. For several decades, he spearheaded protest against the construction of a dam at Tehri on the Ganges in Northern India. His own hut was submerged in December 2001 when the reservoir inundated the poorest quarters of the town. The homes of all its 10,000 population will eventually go under. Thousands of acres of fertile land will also be flooded, displacing 100,000 people. The dam is close to a seismic fault capable of unleashing earthquakes measuring 8.5 on the Richter scale. If it breaches, there will be an immense catastrophe. Despite recommendations from several government reviews that the dam should not be built, its construction has been unstoppable. If previous Indian experience is anything to go by, the outlook for most of those affected is likely to be ruin. Land compensation is restricted by bureaucratic fiat, and much of the cash compensation allocation has already mysteriously disappeared.[2]

Stories such as these abound in most corners of the developing world. Many never see the light of international attention because they are about less spectacular installations – factories, power plants, flyovers, office blocks, fancy new housing developments where villages or settlements of 'illegal' squatters fringed the city and got in the way. Planning does not include democratic consultation, omits adequate compensation for the displaced, and neglects environmental concerns. Construction is accompanied by official secrecy, deal-fixing, corruption and inefficiency – and dirt-cheap wages for site laborers, many of whom are women and children. Not all such projects demonstrate these failings, but they are typical of many. International investment – from the private market, the public purse, or some combination of the two – is often involved.

The irony of these projects is that they are justified in the name of 'development'. This amorphous term covers a host of activities as both means and ends, but unquestionably includes infrastructural projects. In many ways, these are emblematic of development – its symbols, its markers, its statements of faith and in some cases its all-too-familiar white elephants. The essence of 'development', as most people understand the term, is that it should combat poverty. Yet many of these projects adversely affect poor people and inflict poverty on others who were not poor before. They do this in the name of progress, modernization and economic growth – legitimate goals no doubt. But not without legitimate democratic consultation and just compensation.

Development destruction

According to one estimate, 10 million people a year worldwide suffer forced displacement from the construction of dams and urban transportation systems alone.[3] The numbers compare to the 12 million refugees annually displaced by wars and other 'disasters'. But refugees may one day go home. The development-displaced can never do that. Balakrishnan Rajagopal, a human-rights specialist at Massachusetts Institute of Technology in the US, describes these forced dislocations of people as 'development cleansing'. He points out that they may also constitute ethnic cleansing in disguise, since a disproportionate number of the dispossessed are from minority groups. No one knows how many millions of people altogether have been displaced into poverty by large projects: they are systematically undercounted. In China's Western Poverty Reduction Project in Quinghua, the World Bank later discovered that entire towns of Tibetan and Mongol minorities were not counted as 'affected'.[4] According to the World Commission on Dams, up to 80 million people around the world have been displaced by large dams alone.

In fact, many of the projects that precipitate displacement turn out to have been over-optimistic in their cost-benefit projections, and while they may corral rivers, generate power, house civil servants, or enable planes to land, they also contribute to the load of debt under which the country staggers. As a consequence, extra national resources have to be spent on paying back creditors instead of on the education, health, water supplies, livelihood support and basic services the poorest people so desperately need.

Truly, development is a very contradictory affair if it reinforces the very poverty that it aims to eliminate. How can something pursued in the name of 'the poor', to bring about improvements in their productivity and lifestyles, be co-opted to discriminate against them? The reality is that, too often, the poverty of certain communities or nations is used as a pretext for promoting investments that are primarily designed to improve incomes and lifestyles for the better off. This is achieved by creating low-waged employment in burgeoning cities whose buckling urban fabric is another manifestation of acute development distress.

Today, after 50 unprecedented years of rapidly growing global prosperity, 2.8 billion people worldwide survive on less than $2 a day[5] – a greater number than the entire world population in 1950. Instead of creating a more equal world, five decades of 'development' have produced a socio-economic global apartheid: small archipelagos of wealth, within and between nation-states, surrounded by impoverished humanity.[6]

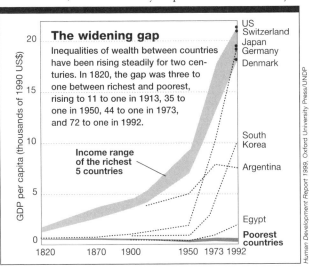

The widening gap

Inequalities of wealth between countries have been rising steadily for two centuries. In 1820, the gap was three to one between richest and poorest, rising to 11 to one in 1913, 35 to one in 1950, 44 to one in 1973, and 72 to one in 1992.

Income range of the richest 5 countries

GDP per capita (thousands of 1990 US$)

US
Switzerland
Japan
Germany
Denmark

South Korea

Argentina

Egypt

Poorest countries

1820   1870   1900   1950 1973 1992

Human Development Report 1999, Oxford University Press/UNDP

In a world where extremists act out their hatred of the 'developed' in stupendous acts of terrorist atrocity, to say that the vision has soured is a gross understatement. The attacks on the US on 11 September 2001 gave a new complexion to the continually evolving relationship between the world's haves and have-nots. So do the escalating protests about globalization, and the new politics of people's resistance in countries such as Mexico and India, where development has been too often experienced not as opportunity, but as damage.

So is the vision of development just a chimera? Should the mission cease? If the activities carried out in its name are so fraught with contradiction and even constitute a pretext for violence against people living in poverty, is the idea of 'development' any longer useful? How do we come to terms with the reality that actions taken at the international level in the name of 'the poor' may do something for a country's balance sheet and for some of its inhabitants, but nothing at all for those whose conditions of life justified it in the beginning? There are painful questions at the heart of this vast and elusive subject.

Beginnings

The idea of development was born not in the developing world, but in the West, as a product of the post-colonial age. Latin American scholars made an important intellectual contribution from the start. The ideas of Mahatma Gandhi of India, Mao Zsedung of China, Julius Nyerere of Tanzania and, more recently, of increasing numbers of actors and thinkers in the countries of the South, also played their part. Nonetheless, its evolution in theory and practice has been driven by the industrialized world.

Today there is a large literature on theories of development, all grist to the mill of development discourse and proof of its academic respectability. Some authors seek the roots of the idea in Marx and Hegel, others go back to 17th century political economist Adam

Smith, or further back to the European Age of Enlightenment with its novel suggestion of transforming the world by scientific discovery and human intervention.[7] One or two even cite the dawn of settled agriculture 10,000 years ago as the moment the development train left the station.

Fascinating as these philosophical excursions into the past are, for all practical purposes the idea in its modern guise came from US President Harry S Truman. On 20 January 1949, in his inaugural address, he declared that the benefits of scientific advance and industrial progress must be made available for the 'underdeveloped' areas. 'What we envisage,' he said, 'is a program of development based on the concepts of democratic fair dealing.'[8] The 1947 US Marshall Plan for economic regeneration in post-Second World War Europe had been a great success. No doubt Truman had something similar in mind for the rest of the world. The underlying purpose, as with the Marshall Plan, was the consolidation of US influence in places that might otherwise be infected with the communist virus.

During the 1950s, the stakes rose. The growing stand-off between Western allies and the Eastern bloc, and the accelerating departure of the imperial powers from their colonies in Africa and Asia, reinforced the strategic urge to lock 'emerging' nations all over the world into the US sphere of influence. Many of the newly independent countries tried to stay aloof. A movement of 'non-aligned' countries was launched in 1955 at a

Naming names

All terms used to denote countries needing 'development' have shortcomings. Axis descriptors – developing/developed, non-industrialized/industrialized, rich/poor – are crude and value-laden. Since the end of the Cold War, the term 'Third World' has become outdated, though it is still sometimes used. 'North' and 'South' are preferable since they carry fewer pejorative connotations. In this Guide, all these terms are used in different contexts, in full recognition that none is satisfactory. ∎

conference in Bandung, Indonesia. Its leaders were the then-giants of the new nations – Presidents Nehru of India and Nkrumah of Ghana, for example. This was the genesis of the 'Third World': an attempt to assert a group identity separate from both the capitalist West – the 'First World' and the Communist Eastern bloc – the 'Second'. As a geopolitical entity, the Third World never stood a chance. But that was not obvious at the time.

A post-colonial construct

As decolonization gathered pace, a new vocabulary was coined to describe free and sovereign countries that had, until then, consisted of imperial subject peoples. The rush for independence – no less than 17 countries in Africa first raised their flags in 1960 – put the seal on the construct of a 'developing' world, with which the Third World soon became synonymous. Apart from the geographical accident that placed almost all the new countries in the tropics, they had an obvious feature in common: their lack of industrialization – in a word, their 'poverty'. To shed this condition, they needed capital resources and technical know-how from what were now their richer 'partners' on the world stage. If the First World was ungenerous, they would – and did – naturally look to the Second.

Thus was born the push for international development, a concept which embraced ideological fervor along with more conventional notions of investment and technological transformation, and a vital part of whose impulse was the strategic and economic self-interest of the US and its allies. Countries that wanted to benefit from Western largesse adopted its language and ideas, even though this cast them and their peoples in pejorative terms as 'ignorant' and inferior, objects of paternalistic assistance.

A crude dichotomy of 'developed' and 'developing' nations had emerged, later re-formulated as North and South. The notional lumping of countries together in large, essentially imagined, agglomerations seemed to make sense. There had been the colonizers and the colonized. Then the wartime split of Allied and Axis Powers, then the East-West division. Why not a new dichotomy of 'worlds' based on a rich/poor, modern/backward version of reality? The residues of this 'bloc' type of thinking show great tenacity. The European Union (EU) still has special co-operation mechanisms for the ACP – Afro-Caribbean-Pacific – countries, whose only common feature is that they were once colonized by European member states.

The United Nations (UN), founded in 1945, provided a forum in which the new perspective gained strength. The network of UN organizations had been founded in a burst of almost religious faith that the Allied powers – which then included the Union of Socialist Soviet Republics (USSR) – could forestall another global conflagration. During the 1950s, the *raison d'être* of international co-operation for mutual security was severely damaged by the swift division of the Allies into two opposing camps.

The UN therefore sought a broader mission: international co-operation for an assault on worldwide hunger, disease, illiteracy and all the economically and socially disruptive forces, which might lead to international turmoil. This was the task to which the international mechanisms devised in the post-War world – the World Bank, the International Monetary Fund (IMF), the UN's funds and specialized agencies – were now to be devoted.

These mechanisms helped confer on the development mission its international character, providing a set of multilateral bodies through which government resources could be channeled. Unfortunately, they also fostered the illusion that such a thing as 'international development' exists. It does not. Action at the international level is confined to a supporting role, in providing funds and forums in which to carry on debate, much of which is tenuously connected to what is happening to people on the ground. This reality is often ignored by enthusiasts who see international action for development as a be-all and end-all. Given the nature and distribution of power, this can never be the case.

The crusade takes off

The crusade began in the 1960s when US President John F Kennedy launched the UN's Decade of Development in ringing tones: 'To those peoples in the huts and villages of half the globe struggling to break the bonds of mass misery, we pledge our best efforts to help them help themselves… If a free society cannot help the many who are poor, it can never serve the few who are rich.' Kennedy followed up with various initiatives: the Peace Corps, the Alliance for Progress, Food for Peace.

Whatever part was played by self-interest, there was also a heartfelt political commitment to the crusade – not only in the US but in Europe and the Commonwealth too. It echoed powerfully across the whole political spectrum, but especially among the radical young. The rich nations should help the poor not only to gain their allegiance, but – as Kennedy said – 'because it is right'. Due to the growing power of media images, the public in the West were becoming aware for the first time of the existence of mass hunger and suffering in large parts of the world. Shock that most of the world's people lived in penury while a few lived well, seared consciences and captured the public imagination. The moral force generated by this realization held the concept of 'world development' together.

The 'hungry millions' version of underdevelopment was simplistic, even degrading. It was also confused. The victim of starvation and the farmer living in a pre-industrial society were frequently regarded as identical, and his or her image as the visual expression of the 'development' problem. Those in the developing world who saw their societies projected in this way were often offended. And people who lived in self-sufficiency off land, forests, seas and rivers were not 'poor' – except in cash terms. But such niceties were buried. The idea of development became the mainspring of a new popular philanthropy. The Freedom from Hunger campaign, launched by the UN's Food and Agriculture Organization (FAO) in 1960, caught a tide of popular compassion in the West, which was also harnessed to the work of a new breed of charitable organizations such as Oxfam.

The UN Development Decade set a target for every industrialized country: one per cent of Gross National Product (GNP) should be devoted to Official Development Assistance (ODA) or 'aid'. Aid – in the form of transfers of public funds on concessionary terms – had previously been associated with the cultivation of military or strategic alliances. 'Aid' was now to become the instrument of 'development', lending support to struggling economies. To many minds, influenced by charity advertisements with images of starving children, the twin ideas of aid and development were golden with promise. Social justice and the welfare state were to be writ large onto an international canvas and the world made more humane by rearrangements of wealth between nations.

Optimism accompanied the launch of the development crusade to a degree now barely credible. The idea that 'underdevelopment' might be cured by a program of investment in infrastructure and technical expertise was unrealistic in the extreme. To be 'underdeveloped' implied that every form of infrastructure was lacking – not simply physical, but political, institutional, professional, financial and administrative, not to mention systems for health, education and social services. These could not emerge spontaneously, courtesy of a transfer of funds and Western know-how.

On the threshold of the development era, however, over-enthusiasm eclipsed common sense. When the Decade of Development began, the idea that a decade might see the task almost through, fantastic as it now seems, did not then appear so far-fetched. Many a 20th-century miracle had been accomplished in less.

There was a strong desire among progressives in the old colonial powers to expiate the sins of the previous generation by helping to build a more equal world. From the new leaders of the developing world came an equally strong sense of urgency and commitment. At the international level, mechanisms to bring about 'development' had evolved or sprung into being. Political and popular will were flowing.

A tarnished vision

By the end of the 1960s, the vision had begun to tarnish. An international commission was set up under Lester Pearson, ex-Prime Minister of Canada, to conduct a 'grand assize' on the impact of development assistance. In one respect, the Decade had been a success: most developing countries had managed to raise their GNP per capita by at least five per cent. But the inescapable fact was that the new wealth had made little if any impact on the majority of their peoples. A small section had become educated and 'modern'; their fortunes and lifestyles integrated with the Western economic system. But the traditional economy had become downgraded even as the numbers dependent on it swelled. More people were poor than before the mission began.

Reporting in 1969, the Pearson Commission noted that 'the climate surrounding foreign aid programs is heavy with disillusion and distrust'.[9] Clearly, prescriptions both for aid and for development needed to be revised and confidence in the goal re-established. Although Pearson acknowledged that development could not be uniform for countries of disparate size, potential and existing organization, he believed it had certain common features in addition to economic growth: social progress, redistribution of wealth, efficient administration, political stability and democratic participation.[10] There is nothing new under the sun – these are the themes of much contemporary analysis, with 'failed states' – those driven by a combination of political and economic adversity into collapse – to prove his point with a vengeance. Pearson also presciently noted that the aspiration for development might be very different from the perspective of the poor farmer or urban dweller in Africa or Asia compared to that of planners, technicians and bankers devising policies on 'his' (and it often was his rather than her) behalf.

By the 1970s, development had bred an industry of governmental and intergovernmental institutions, university studies programs, specialist researchers, practitioners and charitable programs of every stripe. These generated a lively debate about the nature of development, both as a means and as an end. The question of what it was supposed to solve had also expanded. A demographic explosion was underway and the planet's supply of non-renewable resources was seen to be under stress.

Questions about development became subsumed in a general malaise about industrial society and its threat to the environment. Not only had economic growth conspicuously failed to end poverty, but it was under attack from all quarters.

The search for alternatives

Thus 'disillusion and distrust' served to launch a debate about development alternatives. Thinkers became celebrity gurus, unleashing a maelstrom of ideas and challenging every prevailing orthodoxy. From Latin America came opposition to 'developmentalism', suggesting that poverty was structural and could not be solved by granting a manifest destiny to Western industrialization. Paulo Freire, a Brazilian educator, wrote about unleashing people's own awareness and creativity instead of projecting poverty onto them.[11] In 1973, EF Schumacher, a British economic advisor, reacted against the assumption of power by large impersonal institutions in extensive areas of people's lives, with his proposition that 'Small is Beautiful'.[12] Out of Africa came President Julius Nyerere's philosophy of *ujamaa* or socialist self-reliance. From all points of the compass, the search for alternatives was on.

In the world of theory, an attempt was made to argue the case for social investments as a vital contribution, rather than a drain, on economic productivity. Various formulae were produced: 'Redistribution with growth', with an emphasis on job creation and 'Meeting basic needs', with an emphasis on providing basic services, were two examples. In 1973, Robert McNamara, then President of the World Bank, called for the governments of the developing world to reorient their policies to directly attack the poverty of the poorest 40 per cent of their citizens, and the world's investment machinery to reorient itself to help them. McNamara was one of the few World Bank Presidents to talk as if the situation of poor people, specifically rather than incidentally, matters. So does James Wolfensohn, appointed in 1995.

In the world of practice, the failure of many large-scale schemes supported by official aid showed by contrast the relative success of many small-scale non-governmental initiatives – which bore out EF Schumacher's earthy wisdom. These were regarded in official circles as a humanitarian irrelevancy, of no significance in the grand development plan. This myth lingered long in the bureaucratic and 'professional' mind. By their nature, non-governmental contributions responded directly to people's needs and their inputs were of a kind that their recipients could manage. However, their impacts were too small, dispersed and localized to show up even in sub-national statistics, a fact that underscored their insignificance.

Although the 'development' banner was now fluttering over a diffuse and contradictory collection of enterprises, it was constantly expected to fly higher and wider. Population growth, urbanization, desertification, women's rights, ecological conservation: all were concerns the concept had to embrace. Despite the strains, the cause reached its zenith in the 1970s.

In 1973 came the successful Organization of Petroleum Exporting Countries (OPEC) cartel that hiked oil prices and held the oil-consumers to ransom. It showed a Third World determined to extort more from the First and Second Worlds than the crumbs of aid rich countries were typically prepared to offer.

Buoyed up by this success, the Group of 77 – the developing world's organized expression at the UN – made an attempt by weight of numbers to exert some muscle. Their high tide came at two special sessions of the UN General Assembly in 1974 and 1975, which produced resolutions calling for a New International Economic Order (NIEO). No less a figure than Henry Kissinger, then US Secretary of State, said that the industrialized world was ready to enter negotiations with the developing nations on a restructuring of global financial and trading institutions. But hope withered on the vine. Commodity-based Third World unity was never repeated around any other primary product than oil, and within a few years the proposal for an NIEO sank below the international horizon. Instead, the surplus generated by the oil money bonanza helped to usher in the era of debt.

The concept unravels

Ironically, the OPEC shock was the moment when both the geopolitical concept of a Third World reached its apotheosis, and the construct of a coterminous 'developing' world began to crack. The oil price hike produced a body of super-wealthy Third World states in the Middle East, while setting back development for others elsewhere. They might both be 'backward', but how could the United Arab Emirates, with a per capita Gross National Product (GNP) of $13,000 (1975), belong in the same 'developing' bracket as Pakistan, with a per capita GNP of $130?[13]

By the 1980s, a number of non-oil-rich 'newly industrializing countries' had also taken on the coloring of developed economies. These included the four Pacific 'tigers' (Hong Kong, Singapore, South Korea and Taiwan), and some others in Latin America and Asia, prospering from the globalization of the world economy.[14] Meanwhile in Africa, economies were in decline, food production was unable to keep pace with population growth, and drought and civil conflict were rife. A uniform descriptor for these many conditions as 'developing', not to mention any common prescription for 'development', no longer seemed appropriate. No matter. The terminology and perceptions were indestructible.

Already splintering as a concept, the vision of world development dramatically receded in the 1980s. Recession in the industrialized world reverberated in countries heavily dependent on richer trading partners. In 1982, Mexico suspended interest payments on an accumulating mountain of debt, and sparked off what became a crisis of developing country indebtedness. In 1980, the debts of the developing world stood at $660 billion; by 1990, they had more than doubled

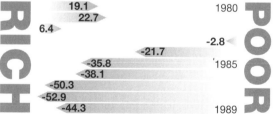

The lost decade

During the 1980s, the transfer of resources from rich world to poor went into reverse, with debt repayments from developing countries eating up and overtaking the inflow of aid, investment and private lending.

Net financial transfers* between donor and recipient countries, $ billions, 1980-1989

Transfers to developing countries

RICH		POOR
19.1	1980	
22.7		
6.4		
	-2.8	
-21.7	1985	
-35.8		
-38.1		
-50.3		
-52.9		
-44.3	1989	

Transfers from developing countries

*'Net transfers' means all loans, long-term and short-term, public and private, minus all interest and capital payments on previous loans.

State of the World's Children 1992, UNICEF and World Bank

to $1,540 billion.[15] No fewer that 60 developing countries experienced declining per capita income over the decade. By its end, the 1980s had become known – especially in Africa and Latin America – as a lost decade, a decade of development reversal.

In the US and Britain, these were also the Reagan-Thatcher years, with the new orthodoxy of market supremacy, reduction of government and attacks on the welfare state, especially the provision of health, education, water, energy and transport by the exclusive agency of government. Lambasted for domestic purposes, the use of public funds for investment in other countries' social and economic infrastructure was way out of line. Under Prime Minister Margaret Thatcher, the UK aid budget was only given the kiss of life when it was pointed out that it was useful for strategic leverage with allies, and that much of it went to the British end of the development industry – UK companies, consultants and academic institutions. Over the decade, aid generally declined.

At the same time, with export earnings hemorrhaging away to pay their debts, an increasing number of developing countries were forced to initiate 'structural adjustment programs' as a condition of IMF loans. Before long the enforced austerity and its human costs were prompting outrage in both North and South. From Tanzania, President Nyerere demanded: 'Must we starve our children to pay our debts?'[16]

The new focus on 'non-state' and 'private' had one important spin-off. The role of voluntary initiative gained new respect. The importance of 'civil society' was much talked up. Both in the North and the South, the activities of a diffuse variety of non-governmental organizations (NGOs) were taken far more seriously. Even if they operated on a localized scale, they were efficient and effective – after all, they were 'private' – service providers. One thing they managed to do, which governments had not, was to reach the poorest sectors of society. That development had failed disadvantaged people was now increasingly obvious. In Africa especially, but also elsewhere, an abyss was being created by the destruction of traditional economic systems and the failure to substitute viable alternatives. In international circles, there was much talk of 'safety nets'. Except from the NGOs on their modest scale, safety nets where they were really needed were nowhere to be seen.

Internationalism in crisis

The end of the Cold War, with its triumphant endorsement of global capitalism, was heralded by the writer Francis Fukuyama as the 'end of history'. It was certainly the end of any coherent 'Third' or 'developing' world, however tenaciously this idea and its corollaries persist.

Today, the aid industry is still intact, dispensing around $55 billion every year in a climate of increasing global crisis.[17] The HIV/AIDS epidemic has claimed 30 million lives, mostly in Africa. Ethnic and religious tensions, previously kept in check by the stasis of superpower stand-off, have blown nations apart. The Asian economic miracle ground to a halt. In spite of a

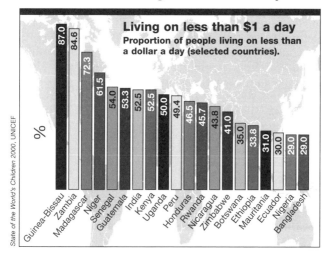

Living on less than $1 a day
Proportion of people living on less than a dollar a day (selected countries).

%

Country	%
Guinea-Bissau	87.0
Zambia	84.6
Madagascar	72.3
Niger	61.5
Senegal	54.0
Guatemala	53.3
India	52.5
Kenya	52.5
Uganda	50.0
Peru	49.4
Honduras	46.5
Rwanda	45.7
Nicaragua	43.8
Zimbabwe	41.0
Botswana	35.0
Ethiopia	33.8
Mauritania	31.0
Ecuador	30.0
Nigeria	29.0
Bangladesh	29.0

State of the World's Children 2000, UNICEF

special debt relief initiative, many heavily-indebted poor countries still languish impecuniously, diverting $59 million daily to much richer governments and financial institutions.[18] Around 1.2 billion people live in direst poverty, surviving on less than $1 a day.[19]

Internationalism is itself in crisis, its mechanisms spawning ever more analyses, prescriptions, conferences and 'poverty reduction strategies', with demonstrably little to show for themselves where it actually matters. There are, to be sure, large numbers of people in the old developing world – 200 million in India, 300 million in China, for example – who newly aspire to a Westernized consumer lifestyle and can afford something approximating to it. They are the purchasers of goods – television sets, computers, electronic goods, branded sportswear – which trade liberalization has brought to their shores. But those living in poverty, when they are asked – as were 60,000 in recent studies commissioned by the World Bank – almost without exception say their situation is deteriorating.[20]

In documents such as the British Government's 2000 White Paper on aid, globalization is held up as the means to assist the poor, despite the fact that it has promoted the exclusion of the poorest sectors of society from any economy that serves their needs. 'We want our lands and our freedom,' says the Mexican farmer confronted by the concrete expression of 'development' – an airport – invading his livelihood system. But he will almost certainly be forced to give up self-sufficiency and an independent way of life to become a lowly servant of others, grateful for a pittance of a daily wage. It is a predicament familiar to around 100 million people displaced by large projects over the last decade, and to countless others similarly expelled to the margins in the name of someone else's progress.

Despite the gloomy picture, or because of it, whatever the record of 'development', this is not the moment to abandon the vision of a fairer world it was invented to create. If machinery exists to address 'world poverty', optimism insists that it be put to better use. The fragmentation the concept has progressively undergone may itself contain the key to a more rational approach. During the 1990s, it accumulated certain qualifiers. One of these was 'human' development, a definition formally combining criteria of both social and economic advance. Another was 'sustainable' development, embracing the need to conserve natural resources. A third was 'participatory' development, echoing the post-Cold War concern with democratization and human rights. In the subsequent chapters of this guide, thinking and practice in such categories are examined to see if they shed light on how to revive the vision.

Development dichotomies

There are other dichotomies to explore. One is the relationship between aid – or 'development co-operation' – and the process it exists to support. Is aid worthwhile? If so, for what kinds of activity? Another is the gap between things done in the name of 'the poor', and what they themselves think should be done. Their voice is insufficiently heard in the development discourse however much lip-service is paid to 'participation'. Many observers have seen the recent growth of people's movements against the relentless homogenization of economies and cultures in a grand global corporate scheme as a manifestation of 'empowerment' and a rejection of the type of development that has caused so much pain. Others see it as a Luddite sabotage of the prescription for global success.

A final introductory issue: what actually is a 'state of development'? As a process, development implies change for the better – in the individual's circumstances as in society's. It is worth noting that humankind only started contemplating such a vision two centuries ago, and even now some pocket-sized societies still endure without any such aspiration.[21] But change towards what? What constitutes the developed society or person? The question begs many others: what is the nature of the poverty this development is supposed to dispel? Many people living off the world's lands or forests without the benefit of modern amenities or cash in their pockets do not perceive themselves as 'poor'. Their aspiration is not necessarily a simulacrum of modern Western consumer society. Thankfully, because if it were, many are destined for permanent exclusion.

What then is the vision of the future to which the people at Tehri, at Atenco – the people themselves, not those who claim governance over them – aspire? Does it inexorably clash with the 'developed' life that those of us equipped to read this book expect to enjoy? And if so, could any version of development be proposed which would keep both sets of dreams intact?

1 Jo Tuckman @ San Salvador Atenco (diary piece), *The Guardian*, 14 January 2002. **2** 'Going Under' Kushal PS Yadav in *Down to Earth*, Vol 10, No 16, CSE, New Delhi, 15 January 2002. **3** Michael M Cernea, World Bank, speaking at a 1995 conference at Oxford University; quoted in *Everybody loves a good drought,* P Sainath, Penguin India, 1996. **4** 'The violence of development', Balakrishnan Rajagopal, *Washington Post*, 9 August 2001. **5** *Attacking Poverty*, World Development Report 2000-2001, The World Bank. **6, 7** *The Myth of Development*, Oswaldo de Riviero, Zed Books and others, 2001. **8** 'Development' in *The Development Dictionary*, Gustavo Esteva, ed Wolfgang Sachs, Zed Books, 1995. **9** *Partners in Development: Report of the Commission on International Development,* Praeger, 1969. **10** *The Crisis of Development*, Lester Pearson, Robert C Leffingwell lectures for the Council of Foreign Relations 1969, Pall Mall Press, 1971. **11** *Pedagogy of the Oppressed,* Paulo Freire, Penguin, 1973. **12** *Small is Beautiful: A study of Economics as if People Mattered,* EF Schumacher, Blond and Briggs, 1973. **13** *Age of Extremes: The Short Twentieth Century,* Eric Hobsbawm, *1914-1991,* Michael Joseph, 1994. **14** *The End of the Third World: Newly Industrializing Countries and the Decline of an Ideology*, Nigel Harris, Penguin, 1990. **15** UNICEF Office of Social Policy and Economic Analysis, Memorandum, 28 June 1995. **16** *Children First: The Story of UNICEF*, Maggie Black, Oxford University Press and UNICEF, 1996. **17** *The Reality of Aid: An Independent Review of Development Cooperation,* Earthscan, 1997-98 **18** *HIPC – flogging a dead process,* Jubilee Plus, September 2001. **19** *Attacking Poverty*, World Development Report 2000-2001, The World Bank. **20** *Voices of the Poor: Crying out for Change,* Deepa Narayan, Robert Chambers, Meera K Shah, Patti Petesch, World Bank, 2000. **21** *Visions of the Future,* Robert Heilbroner, Oxford University Press, 1995.

2 Aid: the international contribution

Aid is the international arm of development. Rich countries have always been niggardly with the amount they give, but the key issues are to do with purposes and methods, not quantity. Aid has been heavily criticized due to the ways it has been squandered, but so many things are done under its umbrella that it is impossible to take a definitive view about its value. Throughout its history, aid has been driven by the donor agenda and relatively little has been used to address poverty, but without it poor countries would be even worse off. Non-governmental aid also has its critics, but it is more likely to address poverty and support alternative development models.

AT THE TIME when 'aid' was invented, the central role envisaged for it in development meant that instrument and purpose were seen as indistinguishable. Aid on a massive scale, furnished by the industrialized world led by the US and the ex-colonial powers, would fuel a 'big push', enabling development in poor countries to take off.[1] In the great majority of nations, this never took place. One problem was that the scale envisaged for aid or official development assistance (ODA) never materialized. Even the targets set – one per cent of industrialized countries' GNP in the 1960s, and 0.7 per cent in the 1970s – were unambitious and could never have accomplished the goal.

Governments signed up to the 0.7 per cent target, but even this has never been met, except by the Scandinavians and Dutch. Although the quantity of ODA provided down the years remains an issue because it is so miserly, this is far less significant than issues associated with its quality and purposes.

The existence of aid created a new sub-set of international affairs, casting developed and developing

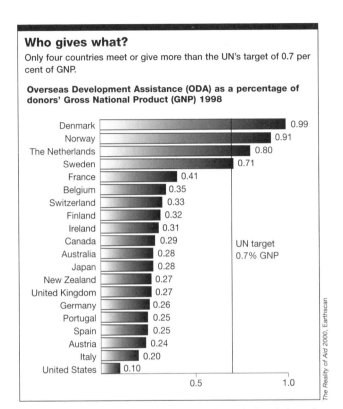

Who gives what?

Only four countries meet or give more than the UN's target of 0.7 per cent of GNP.

Overseas Development Assistance (ODA) as a percentage of donors' Gross National Product (GNP) 1998

Country	ODA % of GNP
Denmark	0.99
Norway	0.91
The Netherlands	0.80
Sweden	0.71
France	0.41
Belgium	0.35
Switzerland	0.33
Finland	0.32
Ireland	0.31
Canada	0.29
Australia	0.28
Japan	0.28
New Zealand	0.27
United Kingdom	0.27
Germany	0.26
Portugal	0.25
Spain	0.25
Austria	0.24
Italy	0.20
United States	0.10

UN target 0.7% GNP

The Reality of Aid 2000, Earthscan

countries respectively as 'donors' and 'recipients'. This relationship, in which the donors are in the driving seat no matter how much this is glossed over with words such as 'partnership', has helped to perpetuate an axis of superiority and inferiority. The implication is that 'development' is a phenomenon exclusive to poor countries – something qualitatively different from economic or social advance in the industrialized world, even though poverty is not confined to the South. And in defiance of common sense, the idea is conveyed to donor populations that Southern poverty is so glaring that, unlike poverty in their own societies, it will be easy to sort out by spending money on it.

The justification for aid, from the outset, has been poverty statistics in developing countries. There is today a huge array of comparative data, much of it collected and synthesized courtesy of 'development assistance'. This is most easily accessed in the World Bank's annual *World Development Report* and the UN Development Program's (UNDP) *Human Development Report.* Some poverty data are expressed in economic terms – GNP per capita, for example; some in social terms – rates of infant mortality, malnutrition, illiteracy; yet others are indicators associated with access to services: family planning take-up, female education, access to health care, safe water and so on. Thus a 'world' picture of needs is conveyed. But whether aid budgets and programs respond to these needs is another matter.

Aid as compensation?

The connections between aid and poverty eradication have always been tenuous. Much aid has been used to help countries compensate for their underdeveloped status in ways that have nothing to do with poverty, tiding them over with advice, specialized expertise and subsidized contracts for high-tech investments, until the notional day when they become developed and can do these things for themselves. The primary purpose of ODA has been to assist the growth of national economies, thereby increasing the grand global total of 'modern' consumers.

It was clear from the start that aid would be used by donor countries for strategic and political purposes and to promote trading ties. But there a set of international bodies existed – World Bank, the International Monetary Fund (IMF) and the UN – through which aid could be channeled on the basis of politically neutral criteria. Their mission: to transfer resources and know-how in the interests of economic and social advance. This was set within the broader framework of international efforts to secure peace and would be free of self-interest, although governing bodies reflected prevailing structures of power, wealth and orthodoxy in financial and economic affairs. This was the climate in which aid was born. With the successful experience of the Marshall Plan for European recovery fresh in every mind, no-one worried that aid would not achieve its purpose. Aid and development were immutably harnessed. One followed the other as night follows day.

This idea of aid as instrumental in development has been extraordinarily tenacious. This is because aid and the institutions associated with it, from the mighty international funds and banks to the smallest charitable endeavor, are the principal international expression of humanity's commitment to the development mission. Without these bodies and the many types of transfers they provide, development would be entirely a local affair, controlled by a recipient country's administrative policies and budgetary investments and bolstered by voluntary and philanthropic activity in the society concerned. The 'international community' in the form of donor agglomerations would have no say over a country's financial, economic, agricultural, health, water resources, education, or any other policy. Because aid has given development an international dimension and the character of a global crusade, and because ODA packages have been used as a lever for all kinds of policy impositions, the concepts of aid and development are difficult to disentangle.

However, it is important to recognize that much international aid has a remote relationship with anything recognizable as development. Much of it never goes near the Southern countries at all. Some is spent on debt relief; some on international bureaucracies based in donor countries; some on vast displays of international discussion. Even a significant component of 'program aid' – that spent directly on activities in developing countries – goes on personnel and machinery set up to administer it, much of which belongs to donors.

Aid may be international, but in the end whether it is effectively connected to development is decided by what happens on the ground. This is largely governed by the behavior of recipients – government ministries and organizations. Developing country bureaucracies typically suffer from many shortcomings: lack of capacity, lack of democracy, lack of efficiency and lack of outreach to the poor. Thus even program aid may be relatively impotent in controlling its results.

Development is subject to many influences, not all of which aid can or should control. Change and progress can happen without the intrusion of aid, and much ODA has failed to make a useful contribution.

Great expectations

Since a lot was expected of it and it has funded many failures, aid has had a checkered history. Early assumptions about the ease with which underdevelopment would give way to the application of aid on a Marshall Plan model soon collapsed. The situation in Africa, Asia and Latin America was quite different from that in post-War Europe, where there had been huge destruction and human distress, but there was an educated population and know-how of all kinds. Once countries had reconstructed, they could put their human capital instantly to work. But in the South, it was a question of building a modern infrastructure for the first time. Most African and Asian countries had no educated cadre waiting to run it – except for the handful of people trained up by the ex-colonizers for purposes of their own. Development could not simply be slapped down upon pre-industrial societies courtesy of aid. Except for the business of commodity extraction via mines and plantations that the colonizers had come for, an autonomous modern economy and the institutions to run it had to be created, mostly from scratch. This is a task requiring generations, and using investment to speed it up has been a puzzle ever since.

The naivety of early aid policy meant that many ventures failed in spectacular fashion. One of the most notorious was an attempt to mechanize agriculture in

Tanzania, Uganda and Zambia that left a trail of abandoned tractors littering the landscape. There were rapid breakdowns, no spare parts, misuse for private purposes, a failure to recover cultivation costs and endless other problems.[2] Many attempts at modernization and industrialization ran into similar disaster. Sophisticated industrial plant and showpiece constructions – which were what most developing countries wanted, not some second-class, bargain basement version of development – quickly fell into disrepair. It became clear that aid would have to be better targeted to help those living in poverty. Unfortunately there were very few structures to manage the use of aid for this.

The criticisms leveled at aid's poor results provided a cast-iron excuse to keep ODA budgets low. But the assumption remained that aid could and would produce development if project quality and performance improved. Within the aid industry itself, the crisis of confidence stemming from early disasters led to a process of re-appraisal. In order to be able to apply aid better to its purpose, development in all its aspects – objectives, strategies, policies – as well as the associated practical arts and sciences – data collection, planning, project design and performance monitoring – were increasingly put under scrutiny. Whatever else it has or has not done since the early fiascoes, aid has since paid for a thorough debate about itself.

Members of the profession insist that the record is not as bad as it is cracked up to be. And ODA has achieved some striking successes. It facilitated the transfer of agricultural technology that brought about the expansion of food production known as the Green Revolution (although this is seen as a mixed blessing in terms of its effects on small and marginal farmers). Aid has also helped to effect major advances in public health, including smallpox eradication, the control of many infectious diseases and significant reductions in mortality and illiteracy. Assistance provided by non-governmental organizations (NGOs) has helped bolster the growth of civil society, and enabled organized expressions of citizen need to bring about improvements in their lives, albeit on a mini-scale.

A variety of critiques

Nevertheless, aid has not been the engine of development originally anticipated. Nor has it brought an end to poverty. And because it appears not to have achieved very much, aid has come in for devastating critique. One school of thought derides it all as damaging, because it creates dependency, fattens bureaucracies and inhibits political dynamics in receiving countries. ODA is also accused of promoting an agenda that exclusively serves the better off, helping élites feather their own nests in league with international business interests.

Another school of thought points to aid's poor results in economic terms and the way it has frequently been filched or squandered. Some analysts look at the correlation between provision of aid to developing countries and their rates of economic growth, and finding no discernible connection, dismiss aid as pointless – or since they are usually themselves part of the aid industry, call for 'reform'.[3] One recent influential treatise from an economist who spent 16 years at the World Bank suggested that there was nothing to show for the $1,000 billion aid disbursed since 1950 as living standards in many parts of Africa and South Asia are lower than 30 years ago.[4] This ignores the good things aid has done, and the fact that there have been many external and internal shocks – economic crises, wars, droughts, famines, HIV – which aid has mopped up. What would have happened without it?

The critiques take in the nature and modalities of development, but much of the opprobrium is pinned onto aid. This seems irrational. It proceeds from the faulty assumption that everything done with aid is similar, pursued for identical purposes; it also confuses the donors' spending policies with the implementation of development policies by recipients. A question repeatedly asked is: 'Does aid work?'[5] The question makes no sense. 'Aid' is a transfer of resources on concessionary terms, or a gift, to be applied to some objective in a developing country. Apart from having this very broad purpose and a corresponding existence as a budgetary umbrella, aid has little generic character. Different types of 'aid' support a vast range of activities, especially if voluntary contributions are included. One would not ask: 'Does investment work?'

Unhelpful messages

Whether aid contributes to socio-economic improvement for disadvantaged people depends on who spends the money and on what. Anyone who has spent time on aid-financed projects knows that the process of intervening usefully in how people conduct their lives is fraught with difficulty. It is hard enough in one's own community; how much harder in societies with quite different political, economic, social and cultural dynamics. Neat constructs of success and failure – which aid organizations dependent on support in donor countries are guilty of perpetrating – rarely apply.

Projects that can be fiercely criticized on one set of grounds – wrong technology, over-optimistic timescales and wasteful extravagance – may also have excellent attributes. Others that are impressive – dynamic leadership, local commitment and visible improvements – may collapse later because of a technical problem no-one could have envisaged. A classic example is the adoption of handpump-tubewells as the universal device for village drinking water in Bangladesh, supported by UNICEF, the UN Children's Fund. When the water table dropped because sources were over-pumped for irrigation, arsenic contaminated the groundwater. A program heralded a success for 20 years was now roundly criticized. Yet no-one could have reasonably anticipated the arsenic problem, nor did the extraction of water for drinking cause the problem. No judgement about 'success' or 'failure' can be guaranteed over time, nor extrapolated from local, constantly changing circumstances. To make a definitive judgement about aid's contribution to development is impossible.

There are many other examples of messages that convey over-simplified ideas about ODA, both to talk up its humanitarian credentials and gather political support, and to talk it down as a waste of taxpayers, money. Just as it is invidious to seize on examples of bad aid investments to dismiss the whole enterprise, it does not help to inflate the case for it on spurious grounds. Aid's supporters continue to evoke the inappropriate model of the Marshall Plan, as with the New Partnership for Africa's Development (NEPAD) initiative promoted at the G-8 meeting in Canada in 2002. Exaggerated claims are made about what could be accomplished to end poverty if official aid flows were nearly doubled from their current level to around $100 billion a year. There is no reason to assume, given the spending policies of many donor and recipient countries, that larger flows would in themselves perform alchemy on poverty in the South. Well-informed observers estimate that, at best, one-quarter of official development assistance reaches people who are poor.[6] Even this estimate seems generous.

The 'aid industry' is an intrinsic part of the machinery of development since it supports and influences it, but it is not the same thing. Yet such is the abiding power of the 'aid = development = poverty reduction' idea, and the hope for humankind that it contains, that simplified equations about the causal relationship between these three phenomena are repeated without serious challenge. They do not help an understanding of what aid is or how it works.

The machinery of aid

The machinery of official aid is not designed to address the poverty of people, but the state of nations.

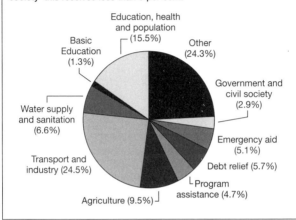

What is aid spent on?

About 25 per cent is spent on transport and industry; over 15 per cent on education and health; and around 6 per cent on debt servicing. Despite all the recent talk about 'governance and civil society' this receives less than 3 per cent.

- Education, health and population (15.5%)
- Basic Education (1.3%)
- Water supply and sanitation (6.6%)
- Transport and industry (24.5%)
- Agriculture (9.5%)
- Program assistance (4.7%)
- Debt relief (5.7%)
- Emergency aid (5.1%)
- Government and civil society (2.9%)
- Other (24.3%)

The Reality of Aid 2000, Earthscan

The international institutions – banks, UN agencies, funds and commissions – and the country-to-country bodies such as USAID and the UK's Department for International Development (DfID), are a constellation of bureaucracies whose only common feature is that they spend money collected from taxpayers in richer countries in countries that are poorer. Whatever the diverse members of this 'international donor community' are most akin to – research institutes, consultancy firms, sub-departments of foreign affairs or boards of trade – they are in no sense charitable bodies writ large. The only part-exceptions are those with a humanitarian mission.

Unlike international NGOs, whose recipients' selection is determined on the basis of their disadvantage, official aid bolsters activities conducted by governments. Some is nowadays also spent through NGOs, but this is a small proportion.

The projects or programs supported by ODA fall

under sectoral headings – finance, planning, agriculture, health – and are intended to bring about economic growth or fill in technical gaps. The assumption is that successful schemes will create jobs, improve crop yields, harness power and improve local capacities in a variety of fields including health and education. Around a third of such aid comes in the form of 'technical co-operation': a euphemism for highly paid experts whose skills recipient countries lack. The condition of people in poverty is rarely tackled by these forms of aid, although they may help draft policies that are meant to address such needs, and some projects are located in poorer parts of the country.

The large salaries and benefits enjoyed by expatriate internationals paid out of official aid attract much adverse comment. But specialists employed by the donor community, including those from the South, are part of the economy of the donor world and are employed at its rates. The resulting inequity is a reflection of the imbalance between the economies of the industrialized world and the economies in which the vast majority of people in the South live. These experts

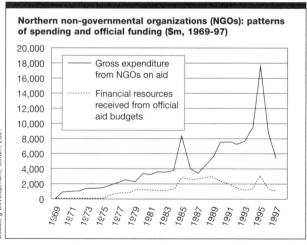

Northern non-governmental organizations (NGOs): patterns of spending and official funding ($m, 1969-97)

Gross expenditure from NGOs on aid

Financial resources received from official aid budgets

Debating Development, Oxfam, 2001

are primarily answerable to the donor bureaucracies, not to the societies in which they serve.

The donor agenda

The idea that newly created wealth automatically trickles down from immediate beneficiaries to the rest of society has long been discredited. Nonetheless, many donor programs still operate according to the old ideology, as if it was axiomatic that 'every transfer helps'. This has fostered an accountancy version of aid, in which the donors' role is to help plan state-of-the-art programs, and then see that the sums of money allocated are properly accounted for to their providers.

Project reports are about the progress of disbursement for planned activities, not about effectiveness. A special language of reportese does little more than repeat stated objectives and plans, as if 'rolling out' the program has of itself achieved the desired result. Many reports to donors are emollient in the extreme; they are needed for audit purposes, not to assess program impact. That is done later by 'evaluation' and has little to do with making a project work better – that is usually completed by this stage. It may help the donor decide whether to extend or reduce a particular aid line – watershed management, say, or condom distribution. There is no democratic check on a program's local impact because the constituency to which it is answerable is not its beneficiaries but its progenitors.

There are all sorts of other obvious ways in which development assistance machinery serves the agenda and requirements of donors. In the case of country-to-country aid, spending policies are biased in favor of strategic and commercial interests. The list of recipient countries to which any donor country has given most of its ODA over the years has, with some exceptions, almost invariably reflected these considerations. To take an example, between 1982 and 1987 the UK annually provided from its aid budget the equivalent of $1,075 for everyone in Gibraltar, $7,705 per head to the Falklands/Malvinas, 20 cents per head to India and 0.0037 cents to Cambodia.[7] Israel has been a disproportionate receiver of US aid. France focuses heavily on Francophone Africa, Portugal and Netherlands on their ex-colonies and so on.

Donor countries have been reluctant to apply poverty criteria and spend more aid in lower-income countries as a principle, but the record has improved. There are also many examples of notorious ODA expenditures: in the early 1990s the UK Government spent $351 million on a hydroelectric dam in relatively wealthy Malaysia as part of a major arms contract, which was subsequently found to be an illegal aid expenditure in the British courts.[8] This kind of aid – and there is still a lot of it – is all about building political alliances and opening up lucrative contracts for home-based companies. Even where the principle of poverty-related spending is established for aid, a clash with trading interests, including the sale of armaments, will usually find the donor's policy playing second fiddle.

Even when not used to promote its own interests,

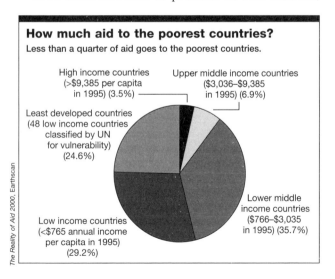

How much aid to the poorest countries?
Less than a quarter of aid goes to the poorest countries.

High income countries (>$9,385 per capita in 1995) (3.5%)

Upper middle income countries ($3,036–$9,385 in 1995) (6.9%)

Least developed countries (48 low income countries classified by UN for vulnerability) (24.6%)

Lower middle income countries ($766–$3,035 in 1995) (35.7%)

Low income countries (<$765 annual income per capita in 1995) (29.2%)

The Reality of Aid 2000, Earthscan

much of any country's ODA is spent on its own cadre of technical experts, and through its own academic, research and consultancy institutions. Even such enlightened donors as Sweden and Denmark still insist that a proportion of their aid budgets be spent on their own products; the proportion spent by the US is 70 per cent.[9] The UK's record has recently improved, trying since 1997 to target aid to poorer countries and spend it on things that correspond to what voters think aid is spent on. But the reality of much aid is still a far cry from the image it carries in the taxpayer's mind. In receiving countries, many representatives of civil society express outrage at the way aid may be used to shore up policies and institutions that entrench poverty, despite its pretence of doing the opposite.

Neutral channels

Much official assistance is spent through multilateral agencies answering to governing bodies made up of representatives from a number of governments, North and South. This is supposed to place them above the squalid considerations of national self-interest dominating bilateral, or government, aid. The most important of multilateral organizations is the World Bank, in terms both of funds and influence; there are also all the diverse UN organizations and many regional bodies. But even though poverty criteria may be applied in their spending policies, their agenda is still largely donor-driven.

For much of its existence, the World Bank has not even pretended to be addressing poverty, mostly supporting a wide range of infrastructural projects: dams, power generation, roads, communications systems. After a brief flirtation with poverty reduction during the 1970s, its main activity became the provision of funds to promote the 'structural adjustment' of developing country economies along free market lines. The social distress these reforms created became so glaring that in the 1990s the World Bank rediscovered poverty as an aid target and introduced country-based 'poverty-reduction strategies'. But whatever the rhetoric, its support has always been used as an instrument for binding countries into economic policies it approves. World Bank reports deeply lament the scale of extreme poverty in the world, but are reluctant to admit that the policies it has espoused bear some share of responsibility.

International non-governmental organizations (NGOs) also belong to the ideology and culture of the donor world, but they do not have another agenda from the one they notionally serve. They have generally been much better than donor governments at spending money so as to enable disadvantaged people to improve their lives. This is the reason that most official aid bodies are now keen to spend through them and local affiliates, thereby supporting 'civil society' – a term currently exercising a mantra-like charm. Not all local or international NGOs are an unqualified good thing. The availability of funds has brought many spurious organizations into existence, and the plethora of agencies has had the unfortunate effect of promoting a begging-bowl mentality.

NGOs make mistakes and some may be unscrupulous. But at their best they are in touch with the myriad realities of people's lives in a way undreamt of among the authors of the macro-policy and the master plan. Some have helped find alternative models of development that better serve the poor. This is not a path along which government and multilateral donors have generally been willing to follow.

After the Cold War

The 1980s can be seen as the nadir of international development co-operation. Recession in the industrialized world, high interest rates, debt and balance of payments crises rained down on poor countries with disastrous consequences. Social expenditures were dumped, and instead came stabilization and painful structural adjustment. The use of aid was subjugated unashamedly to donor agendas, to expanding the global economy, and protecting it from financial risk. The World Bank and IMF pushed a macroeconomic agenda known as the 'Washington consensus', which was all about prudent fiscal and monetary policies, control of inflation, and leaving things to the market. Their loan packages required countries to cut services, depress wages and as a consequence throw millions of people out of work. There was a new emphasis on private flows of capital and on opening up private-public partnerships – often a recipe for private profit by corporations and their allies, and public theft of people's resource base and livelihoods.

During all this, the socially oriented aid organizations battled on. UNICEF ran a successful campaign for universal childhood immunization and the promotion of child rights. NGOs' status and coffers were enhanced in the 1980s and 1990s. Disasters in Africa helped generate a lot more public sympathy in donor countries for people in need than was echoed by the official establishment, which was forced to recognize that its policies had failed to bring about recovery in debt-ridden and economically depressed countries. Africa in particular was disaster-hit, and the most marginal members of society – landless people, abandoned women, children, people with HIV – suffered disproportionately.

When the Cold War ended, great hopes were attached to 'the peace dividend' it would unleash, and images of major transfers of aid to tackle world poverty dangled before the international imagination. In fact, after a peak in 1992, aid budgets were cut: in 1997 they reached an all-time low at an average of 0.25 per cent of GNP.[10] This was mainly to do with the end of ODA's use as a component of Cold War strategy. In the past, development assistance was awarded to any regime friendly to the West, but now there is no strategic reason to do this, although other global politics operate. 'Right policies' became decisive in selecting recipient countries;

the pursuit of the global economic agenda and willing accommodation to that became paramount concerns, with democracy and human rights following behind. Another major change was the disappearance of former Eastern bloc countries as donors, and their re-emergence as recipients, reducing the proportion of aid available for the 'old' developing world.

Targets for 2015

There was also a re-awakening of donor concern that aid should not only be justified in the name of poor people, but should actually be spent in ways conducive to poverty eradication. Over the course of the 1990s, a number of UN conferences were held at which a series of poverty reduction targets was articulated: the number of people living in extreme poverty to be halved, a two-thirds reduction in child mortality, a 50 per cent reduction in hunger and malnutrition, a reversal in the spread of HIV/AIDS, universal primary education, and others.

These targets were affirmed at the UN Millennium Summit in 2000, for achievement by 2015. These goals are now cited as the purpose of increased donor aid. But there is little to suggest that the services that could deliver these improvements could spring into existence if larger aid flows materialize. There is no internationally accepted strategic plan to enable this to happen.

Although much lip service is paid to the need for social investments, in fact there are very few donors who commit more than 10 per cent of official aid to basic health and education expenditures – the average is less than four per cent.[11] Even when they do, all the inhibitions on reaching the really poor – lack of outreach, lack of motivation, bureaucratic inertia – cannot suddenly be overcome because this is what enlightened donors say they want their aid to do. In many settings government personnel still rarely go near poor communities. When they do, few demonstrate empathy, understanding, motivation to make services work.[12]

This does not mean additional aid could not be spent well – on writing off debt, building up government capacity, re-creating security systems where these have broken down, funds for cheap drugs, better data collection and regulatory mechanisms to stop 'development' scams which exploit people and violate their rights. Some of these are current directions in donor policy, but in a relatively minor way. The opportunities for doing them effectively are hard to find, and still the problem remains of how to carry them out through existing administrative structures. In most poor countries these desperately need to be improved, but instead their reduction is often sought as a component of donor-driven 'economic reform'.

The climate improves

In the wake of the attacks on the US on 11 September 2001, the climate for aid has improved. Suddenly, the consequences of extreme alienation associated with poverty have become sufficiently threatening to impinge on donor minds. Recipient countries have been quick to adopt the new rhetoric: 'To speak of development,' said Alejandro Toledo, President of Peru, at the 2002 UN Summit on Global Poverty in Monterrey, Mexico, 'is to speak also of a strong and determined fight against terrorism.'[13] The Summit, from which little was originally expected, produced new commitments to aid: after a decade of decline, the US will boost aid spending by an extra $5 billion a year by 2006; the European Union by $7 billion a year by 2005.

However, the typical post-Cold War ways of spending – on middle-income developing countries keen to join the global economy, and on donors' own hardware, personnel and services – are likely to prevail. The battle to persuade the US administration that aid is not entirely ineffective was only won after an extensive rearguard action by World Bank analysts insisting that they can point to countries – Uganda, Ghana,

Mexico – where recent economic growth can be linked to aid and the leverage over policy reform it produced. So the Bank's recipe for using aid to produce 'right policies' is what will apply, with a new emphasis on crushing dissidents designated as terrorist threats to US-friendly regimes.

It is therefore unlikely that the new aid will reach those who are deeply frustrated, extremely poor, and antagonized by the relentless pursuit of a form of development from which they are excluded. Aid, even in larger quantity, will do little to repair the damage caused by the policies recipient countries are forced to accept. These demand that their markets be opened as a condition of aid, while the donors keep their own markets locked and their borders shut to people fleeing destitution. The fragile modern economies of some countries are near collapse. Millions of the 'very poor' live in failed or 'non-performing' states. It is in these environments that alienation and exclusion flourish, but which most donors – notably the US – do not want to touch, because in them aid will be 'wasted' or not used 'effectively'. According to this view, aid is only useful if it helps bring countries into a global economy, on terms that the dispossessed of the world perceive as their Armageddon.

In the light of all that has been done to their societies by aid and the policy conditions surrounding it, some critics in developing countries would prefer that it ended; it is seen as a humiliating feature of Northern ascendancy. Nepalese commentator Pitamber Sharma accuses aid of systematically corrupting the minds of his country's bureaucrats, planners and politicians[14]. Naila Kabeer, an academic from Bangladesh, would like aid to be limited to humanitarian relief in wars and natural disasters. However, vested aid industry interests would strenuously resist such a move, and it is difficult to believe that declaring a moratorium on aid would really improve matters for poor people. With all its contradictions, the bus will roll on.

As part of the new international reckoning, it would be nice to think that aid could be applied more imaginatively to reducing poverty, but hopes cannot be high. When it comes to the crunch, the donors have been unwilling to recognize that, to deliver on their rhetoric about poverty reduction, they need to promote much more radical agendas. The economy in which the donors operate, and the economy in which the poorest people on the planet live, are so far removed from one another that they barely interconnect. Bridges are needed to cross the gap, as the next chapter will explore.

1 'The evolution of the development doctrine and the role of foreign aid 1950-2000' WW Rostow, quoted in Eric Thorbecke; *Foreign Aid and Development,* ed Finn Tarp, Routledge, 2000. **2** *Mwea: an integrated rice settlement in Kenya,* ed Robert Chambers and Jon Moris, Weltforum Verlag, Munich, 1973. **3** 'Helping Hands', John Cassidy, *New Yorker,* 18 March 2002. **4** *The Elusive Quest for Growth: Economists' Adventures and Misadventures in the Tropics,* William Easterly, MIT Press, 2001. **5** See for example *Does Aid Work?* Robert Casson and associates, Clarendon Press, 1985, revised 1994. **6** *The Poverty of Aid,* David Ransom quoting Hans Singer in *New Internationalist* No 285, November 1996. **7** *Bilateral Aid: Country Programmes*, HMSO 1987; quoted in Graham Hancock, *Lords of Poverty,* New Atlantic Press, 1989. **8** 'Aid for arms scandal' in *New Internationalist* 264, February 1995. **9** *The Reality of Aid 1997-98*, Annual independent review of development cooperation published by Earthscan. **10** *Assessing Aid,* Paul Collier and David Dollar, World Bank, 1998. **11** *The Reality of Aid 2000,* Earthscan. **12** *'Crying out for Change'* Deepa Narayan, Robert Chambers, Meera K Shah, Patti Petesch, Study for the World Bank Development Report *Attacking Poverty,* 2000-2001. **13** 'World Welcomes Poverty Pledges', Charlotte Denny, *The Guardian*, March 22 2002. **14** 'No pain, no gain', Pitamber Sharma, *Nepali Times*, February 2002.

3 Economic development – who benefits?

Development is assumed to be primarily about economic advance, achieved in such a way as to eradicate poverty. But the kind of economies in which many poor people live are actively ignored, and the kind of economic progress that is taking place often deprives them of their livelihoods. Some economic growth, the standard measure of development, is undoubtedly necessary. But too little effort has been made to invest in models for growth that would permit people still living off the natural resource base to maintain security over their means of survival.

ALTHOUGH THE ECONOMIC language in which they are described is universal, different people in different parts of the world live in very different economies. The task of development is often seen as linking these up – enabling those living in 'traditional economies' to join 'the economic mainstream'.

Although there has been integration between the economies of developing countries and those of the industrialized world over the past 50 years, a third of the world's population – around two billion people – still remain outside the modern economy or survive at its edges. The gulf between economies where the main productive activities are typified by herding and petty trading, and those powered by stock markets, transnational corporations and technology, has consistently widened. The modern economy has grown spectacularly during the development era. But far from being enabled to find their niche – their 'comparative advantage' – in a smoothly flowing economic mainstream, that mainstream has driven the once dependable, if limited, economies of millions of people into ruin. Its flood has passed them by, or deposited them like flotsam on its banks.

Growth in the world economy

The world economy has grown dramatically during the past 50 years, both absolutely and per capita, despite population growth.

Gross world product, 1950-2000

Trillion Dollars (1999 Dollars)

Gross world product per person, 1950-2000

Dollars (1999 Dollars)

Vital Signs 2001, Worldwatch Institute

Some of the victims of this exclusion live in states driven into collapse by a combination of political and economic adversity. Take the villagers of Siya Sang, a community perched in the majestic canyons of Jawand district in western Afghanistan. After 23 years of war and four of drought, a father, Rahim Dad, is forced to sell his only remaining asset – his 12-year-old daughter, Aziz Gul – into marriage for $80 to feed the rest of his family.[1] Her fate is not uncommon in an area where hunger is rife, tuberculosis rages and all other available assets – donkeys, goats, oxen, jewelry, family treasures – have perished or been sold already. Thus, the 'failed economy' of the 'failed state' can be one in which the only marketable item left is the servitude of children.

Transactions of this kind – trading girls into marriage occurs frequently in many areas of Asia and

Africa even where starvation is not impending – do not show up in standard economic analysis. Nor do millions of others on which the people living in these economies depend, not to mention inputs to the household economy which are 'free' because they are gathered from the natural environment: water, food, fuel, fodder, housing materials, medicinal plants. The 1.2 billion people who are described as living on less than a dollar a day are kept alive by these contributions and transactions. In fact, that statement is itself an artificial monetarization of livelihoods in an economy where cash transactions via a recognized market are only one, and certainly not the most significant, lubricant from the perspective of those dependent upon it.[2] These economies are invisible to planners and treated by them as if they do not exist. Where they get in the way of the official version of economic advance, they are routinely swept away.

Invisible economies

Within these kinds of economic set-ups, the picture is far from uniform. The local setting and the dynamics of demand and supply within it, as well as social and cultural codes, affect livelihood arrangements. But in most of their settings today the picture is one of shrinking margins, a greater sense of insecurity, the breakdown of traditional social cohesion and increasing difficulty in managing assets of land, water, fuel, grazing and holding onto household reserves such as jewelry and keepsakes.

In rural areas, access to land is key. A family of tribals (*adivasis*) living on the Narmada River in Madhya Pradesh, India, might graze cattle in the forest, plant crops seasonally in the riverbed and lead a comfortable life. When a dam is built and the forest and riverbed submerged, they become destitute. The cash passing through their hands when they were well off compared to now that they are destitute may not alter substantially. Since they never 'owned' land or had title, their economic status may be formally the same. But the livelihood base that they are forced to resort to – the unskilled labor of men gone to town, the scavenging of women – can barely support life. 'Now we eat only the cheapest rice, no pulse, no vegetables, maybe some forest leaves.' And before the submergence? '*Roti* (bread), *dal* (lentils), curds, rice, vegetables, fruits, everything.'[3]

Similar types of resource-base shrinkage are common throughout the South under the weight of economic, political, demographic and environmental pressures including HIV/AIDS. Traces of these collapsing economies turn up fleetingly, in the interstices of crop production or cattle sales, or in the mounting costs to national health or municipal budgets of high epidemic disease tolls or urban crime. They can also be detected in the statistics of economic migration, illegal urban settlement, the numbers of abandoned and widowed women 'heads of household' and growing numbers of children scraping a living on the streets.

These are economic indicators too, but they tend to be seen as social outcomes of something called poverty, not as measures of poverty itself. And they are difficult to count: they occur in a black, or gray, or hidden zone of economic life. As do the growing

Detecting the unmeasurable

A major problem with understanding the characteristics of much social stress is that they are difficult to assess. Figures for street children, prostitution, child labor, trafficking, forced displacement, early marriage, informal trading, casual employment, and marginal incomes are elusive and unreliable. Even data collection for such apparently straightforward things as access to water and sanitation is often heavily flawed. National or state population averages for any indicator obscure localized downward trends and discrepancies among populations. Such is the modern obsession with measurable indicators and synthesized comparative data that what is unmeasurable or unavailable becomes excluded from analysis. This helps reduce the visibility of many groups of disadvantaged people and allows false assumptions to be made about improvements in their lives. ■

numbers of young women – in West Africa, Burma/Myanmar, Thailand and Eastern Europe – being traded into prostitution or domestic service abroad. One of the most shocking characteristics of livelihood shrinkage is the way it has led to increased commodification of women's and girls' nurturing, childbearing and sexual capacities – resources at the bottom of humanity's barrel when there is nothing else to scrape.

Growing inequalities of wealth

This is just a glimpse of the marginalization and social disintegration stemming from growing inequalities of wealth. These have recently become more pronounced both between countries and within them. In 1960, the income gap between the fifth of the world population in the richest countries and the fifth in the poorest was 30 to one; by 1960 it had become 60 to one and by 1997, 74 to one.[4] In 70-80 developing countries, the average income per head is today lower than ten or even 30 years ago.[5]

No-one now disputes that the globalization of the world economy has contributed to this trend, concentrating opportunities and rewards in certain groups while marginalizing others. Although there is no apparent connection between the economic aristocrats of the company boardroom and those who live by carting loads or pounding yams, the effects of corporate decisions still reverberate all the way down from global and national balance sheets to the alleys, huts and shanties where poor people live. Their resource base is reduced, the prices they can fetch for their produce or labor stagnate or decline, while those they pay for essentials rise, and services that used to be free now have to be paid for.

So while the world economy goes on growing and extending its consumerist lifestyle into millions of households, its record of offering opportunity and progress to people who languish at its edges has been disastrous. Yet economic development is central to any significant advance in social well being, and there can be no release from poverty without economic growth. That at least remains the central orthodoxy. And it is difficult to dispute. For one thing, there can be no spread of health and education services in traditional communities such as those in Afghanistan, India and sub-Saharan Africa, without the financial resources to pay for them. But how and where should this economic growth occur? Can it be generated without further eroding the fragile life-support systems of millions of families? If, as currently constructed, it actually prevents them from leading productive and dignified lives, then something needs to change.

The macro-economic talk today is of 'managing globalization in such a way as to reduce poverty'.[6] Can it be done, or does the suggestion contain insuperable internal contradictions? And if it can't be done for those people still dependent on herding goats or forced into selling their 12-year-old daughters, what are the economic prospects for them?

Where did all the growth go?

In the early days of the development mission, there was rapid economic growth. During the 1960s, the goal of 5 per cent increase in GNP in developing countries was on average surpassed.[7] This was achieved mainly by robust commodity prices, for minerals, oil and agricultural export crops around which colonizers had organized their satellite economies; also, especially in Latin America, by trade barriers and boosts to local manufacture to reduce import bills – a growth strategy known as 'import substitution'. Although those concerned about poverty deplored the fact that the new wealth did not 'trickle down', most developing country governments were more worried about keeping up the flow of resources they needed to industrialize, build new capital cities, construct roads, dams and airports, and keep their new élites content.

In the 1970s, the prices for many of their raw materials began to drop. After OPEC's successful hike of oil prices, the Group of 77 tried to negotiate better prices from the industrialized world for other commodities as the basis for a 'new international economic order'. Apart from getting some conferences convened – for example, at UNCTAD (the UN Conference on Trade and Development) – nothing much came of this. Prices for raw materials such as copper, tin, sugar, coffee and tea, on which many were precariously dependent, continued to decline. Many small farmers trying to join the cash-crop economy saw little return for their pains.

Non oil-producing developing countries, especially the poorest, were hard hit by the oil-price rise. Between 1980 and 1991, they lost $290 billion due to lower prices for their exports – but the prices for manufactured goods they had to import continued to rise. The stage had been set for the debt crisis and the end of hopes that many developing countries could ever 'catch up'.

The huge petrodollar windfall accruing to OPEC members ought surely to have been used for productive investment in impoverished neighbors. Here, finally, was the cash – $310 billion between 1972 and 1977[8] – for investment on a massive scale that protagonists for an end to world poverty had sought since the 'big push' began.

Instead, a travesty occurred – a travesty in which Western banks and key financial institutions on the one hand, and Southern dictators and governing élites on the other, colluded. Some of the new wealth went on construction. But much of it wound up as investment in equity markets or was deposited in Western banks. These were desperate to lend, and lend they did to loan-hungry Southern borrowers for a variety of loss-making ventures. Some went into the pockets of corrupt regimes and kleptocrats who, during the Cold War, were immune from standard economic scrutiny if their alliance was valued, and if they bought Western products and services, including arms.

Not productivity but debt

As the debt burden on poor countries grew and bal-
ance-of-payments crises multiplied, the IMF and the
World Bank began to impose stringent conditions on
debtor nations in return for rescue packages.
'Structural adjustment' became the new route to economic health. But the prescription was steeped in the
new orthodoxies of deregulated markets, dismantling
of trade barriers, privatization, the shrinkage of government, and cutbacks in social expenditures that
gained ascendancy in the Reagan-Thatcher era. There
were massive lay-offs in the public sector, unemploy-
ment spiraled, and budgets for health, education and
social safety nets were reduced. Exports to earn foreign exchange were preferred to investment in basic
necessities and domestic food production.

Structural adjustment may have helped salvage the
international banking system, but it did little for struggling local economies and released few countries from
debt. So both debt and the measures imposed for its
redemption served to push poor communities living in
the cracks of the tottering modern economy into
deeper trouble. As the national cake shrank or its
product melted away in debt repayments, poor people's claim on a slice of it declined disproportionately.
If services and livelihood incentives barely reached
them in the past, now they were positively discriminated against. Their vulnerability became acute.

Meanwhile, the new behemoths of economic growth
– the transnational corporations – were getting into
their stride. In the last quarter of the 20th century, they
became the principal designers and controllers of the
economy in which the world's citizens – if they could
afford to – ate, drank, smoked, dressed, drove, played
sports, listened to music and watched TV. In 25 years
the numbers of these corporations grew from 7,000 to
38,000, with 250,000 subsidiaries, spreading an identik-
it lifestyle all over the world.[9] Although a third of the
world's population could not remotely afford to join

The burden of foreign debt

Despite pledges made at the Earth Summit in Rio in 1992, the total debt burden in developing countries has climbed by 34 per cent, reaching $2.5 trillion in 2000.

External debt of developing and former Eastern bloc countries, 1970-2000

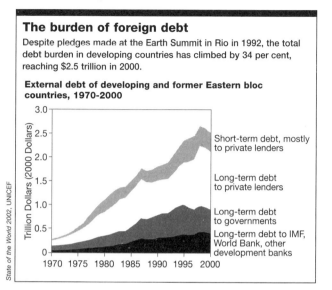

Short-term debt, mostly to private lenders

Long-term debt to private lenders

Long-term debt to governments

Long-term debt to IMF, World Bank, other development banks

State of the World 2002, UNICEF

in, that still left potential markets of hundreds of millions who could. These corporations and their offshoots now conduct two-thirds of the world's trade, and they decide worldwide where, what, how and for whom their products shall be produced. Many are richer – and more powerful – than nation states.

The giant logo-land they promote is the familiar face of globalization, and the part which has been most heralded as improving the economic prospects of the developing world by creating jobs and purchasing power. And although there are many appalled critics of the sweatshop conditions in which clothes, electronic gadgets, toys, computer parts, CDs and a host of other products are made – often in 'export processing zones' where the companies enjoy freedom from taxes and labor regulations – it is hard to make out that they have done nothing at all for people in poor societies. The employment of women in the garment export industry of Bangladesh, for example, has brought them a status and a bargaining position they never enjoyed before.

What also cannot be denied, however, is that the power these companies exert is devoid of moral purpose: the top line and the bottom line are profit, not the advancement of the human condition. Poverty, in the form of rock-bottom wages, is the 'comparative advantage' these environments offer. If labor is cheaper and as malleable elsewhere, if better deals can be cut for tax holidays and the political environment is more secure, the women of Bangladesh will lose their jobs tomorrow. The 'free trade' treaties sponsored by such bodies as the World Trade Organization (WTO) pave the way. So do national authorities keen to bring in the investment.

Another side of the picture is the image of the good life peddled to the next generation of the global market's would-be consumers – that condemns them as second-class citizens. Fantasies of affluence, freedom and power flash via television into the remotest places, opening a window onto a fairytale world, but no door to get there. The global monoculture these images purvey can destroy the values of ancient societies with shocking speed, its busy tentacles reaching into their existing way of life with crushing effect. Their growing familiarity with images of modern life comes with growing awareness of their exclusion. People whose way of life once had self-sufficiency and self-respect become insecure appendages to its embrace, reduced to menial and servile labor at its fringes.

The social anthropologist Helena Norberg-Hodge has written eloquently of the damage wrought by the introduction of money into the subsistence economy of Ladakh (in Kashmir, India) over recent decades. In the 1970s, the existing economy supported a high standard of living compared to that in most shantytowns. Before the arrival of an unstable monetary system, the Ladakhis were not 'poor' at all. Once they accepted meager wages or grew crops for distant markets, they became dependent on forces beyond their control – transport, oil prices, international finance.

'Increasingly, people are locked into an economic system that pumps resources out of the periphery into the center. Often, these resources end up back where they came from as commercial products, packaged and processed, at prices the poor can no longer afford.'[10]

Northern commercial interests lay siege to non-industrialized societies, making indigenous, organic forms of development a near impossibility.

The human price

One other phenomenon of recent times intrinsic to globalization adds to the picture of economic instability and intrusion: the deregulation of global finance. In the 1990s, the IMF and World Bank backed the opening up of financial markets in developing countries as the latest prescription for economic growth. As country after obedient country did as it was told, there was an explosion of currency transactions aided by electronic communications. In 1980, the daily average of foreign exchange trades was $80 billion; today, $1,210 billion changes hands. Virtually none of this has to do with producing goods and services.

Money chasing money in short-term speculation has replaced productive enterprise as the global economic motor. Capital is moved instantly from one market to another, to take advantage of interest-rate differentials, unstable currency values and other virtual margins. The effect is artificial confidence, debt, volatility – and crash. Such a fate befell the Asian 'tiger economies' of East Asia in 1997. Money that had surged in, surged out. Financial crisis led to economic crisis, in which – because of both the capital flight and IMF rescue conditions – those clinging to the tiger's tail were discarded. Around 13 million people lost their jobs and thousands of small businesses went to the wall. By 1998, 75 million more Indonesians lived in poverty than in 1996. Many have yet to recover. They are not alone: in the global casino, Mexicans, Russians and Argentineans have also been losing the shirts off their backs.

The world has become much more prosperous and there has been corresponding economic growth in many developing economies. But its human price is high. In many countries it has created an economic plateau marooned above an ocean of semi-subsistence living, petty entrepreneurship and rock-bottom wages. Those perched on the plateau, enjoying an automobile-and-verandah lifestyle, are much more closely linked to international markets and financial systems than to those who inhabit their own backyards. Exporting inequitable economic development into societies with a deeply entrenched sense of social, ethnic, or caste hierarchy reinforces inequity further. Unless they can sell them Coca-Cola, medicines or cigarettes, or wish to hire them as domestic servants, many of those who have joined the modern world ignore the fate of their socio-economic inferiors.

At one rung up the social ladder – a place which the sons, and occasionally daughters, of upwardly mobile smallholders and tea-stall owners may just have managed to reach – things are not much better. Formal employment opportunities are not expanding: in Latin America over the 1990s, the proportion of jobs in the informal sector rose from 52 per cent to 58 per cent.[11] Such livelihoods are shadowy and undependable.

In many parts of Africa and Asia, those in the lower grades of the public services – clerks, schoolteachers, policemen, health workers – are so badly paid that they are obliged to engage in 'businesses' to keep their families afloat. Many petty functionaries, especially those in remote, under-resourced or conflict-ridden outposts do not receive their salaries for months or years on end. Unsurprisingly, they are not committed to their jobs. If they can escape into the global marketplace, at home or overseas, they do so.

The exclusive model

Meanwhile, senior bureaucrats, politicians and businessmen fix up 'public-private partnerships' – not perhaps in quite the form envisaged by their Northern protagonists – to preserve their joint hold over contracts, markets and budgetary allocations. There is no growth here of a kind in which people with fraying livelihoods can share. On the contrary, since plunder not productivity is usually the name of the game, where they look like potential competitors the poor are systematically cut out.

At the beginning of the development era, there were two available systems for economic organization leading to economic growth: capitalist and communist. The triumph of the capitalist model with its energy-inducing dynamics – its ubiquitous drive for capital accumulation, and its co-option of technology and science in a ceaseless competition for market share – is now part of history. But there has been a

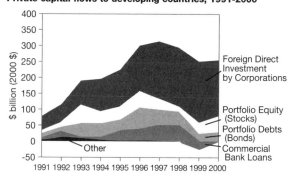

Private investment flows

In recent years, private investments have become the main source of financial supply to countries of the South. They grew by more than five times during the 1990s, from $209 billion to $1,118 billion. Private finance is often compared favorably with aid, but it is a different creature. This source of development finance is entirely profit-based. It mainly goes to economically attractive markets, and often to resource extractive sectors. The poorest countries receive next to nothing: in 1998, they received 0.5 per cent of world financial flows.

Private capital flows to developing countries, 1991-2000

Foreign Direct Investment by Corporations

Portfolio Equity (Stocks)

Portfolio Debts (Bonds)

Commercial Bank Loans

Other

$ billion (2000 $)

1991 1992 1993 1994 1995 1996 1997 1998 1999 2000

State of the World 2002, UNICEF and World Bank.

major problem. The grand development graft from North to South did not take well. It only seems to work when it is conjoined to the global economy and co-opted to its requirements.

Even then, it is often inefficient even on its own terms. Perhaps this is not surprising. The US economist Robert Heilbroner puts it like this: 'The technology and science that entered the periphery came there not as indigenous creations, but as emplacements of foreign hegemony – the fortresses of economic empires. In similar fashion, the capitalism that penetrated into the periphery was exported from abroad rather than nurtured from within, and therefore served to constrict, not to liberate the forces of enterprise in the recipient areas.'[12]

The prime pillars of a healthy economy are deemed by the global financial and trading powers to be a flexible labor market, competitiveness and profitability. When poor people in the South are asked what they find most difficult about life under this regime, two main themes crop up in their replies: insecurity and powerlessness. The economic growth brought about by globalization unnerves and damages them, but is there any choice?

Where small is beautiful

Until the early 1970s, the prevailing belief was that, in time, economic growth would bring prosperity and peace to all. Science and technology had performed so brilliantly in tandem with capital that – whatever new problems were thrown up by humanity's extraordinary behavior and inventiveness – they would ride over the horizon to the rescue. Food shortages? Lo and behold, the Green Revolution. Fossil fuel exhaustion? Here comes nuclear energy. Toxic waste? Just wait, the scientists will soon come up with something. But awareness was dawning that forces were at work that had dramatically changed things.

Since the Second World War, humanity had begun

to consume the earth's supply of non-renewable resources at an alarming rate. Demographic trends – the population 'explosion' became a *cause célèbre* at this time – suggested that the speed of consumption was bound to accelerate. For the first time the prospects of infinite growth appeared doomed. The idea of 'Limits to growth' – the title of a landmark report – was powerful and chilling.

Apart from introducing to a wide audience the concept of an ecological system and the need to preserve its integrity, this thinking was revolutionary because it attacked growth. Growth was not necessarily beneficent – it might even be harmful. The guru of 'small is beautiful', EF Schumacher, wrote: 'The substance of man cannot be measured by Gross National Product.' He went on to decry the chicanery of economics, with its celebration of 'the market' and 'economies of scale'. He deplored the 'idolatry of giantism', and suggested that any system of development which began from quantitative premises instead of where people were already at would be bound to fail. It might also ruin them. In the villages of the developing world, intermediate forms of technology were needed to deploy people's existing skills and meet their real requirements. Schumacher was scorned as a romantic and accused of peddling development, second-class. But his ideas had huge resonance in both North and South.

The attack on growth – not just because it hadn't trickled down, but absolutely – was joined from many quarters. The idea of development from the bottom up was echoed in the 'basic communities' of Brazil, by Tanzania's rural socialist experiment of *ujamaa*, and by village-based development in China. If development were authentically bottom-up, it would produce growth at the community level, but on such a small scale that unless it was replicated thousands of times over this would not be reflected in national Gross National Product (GNP). But in this version of development, that hardly mattered. The livelihoods of people and communities were what mattered. Non-governmental organizations (NGOs) began to promote 'community-based development' and 'self-reliance'. These were later co-opted into development thinking. But they were not taken seriously by the big league or by most governments. Where such ventures were allowed to flourish (some were obstructed), they were disregarded from an economic point of view.

The advent of microcredit

In the 1980s, however, some economic enterprises based on these ideas began to attract attention. In 1974, when Bangladesh was in the grip of famine, Mohamed Yunus, a professor of economics at Dhaka University, visited a village just outside the campus. He was horrified to discover that a woman making bamboo stools earned the daily equivalent of $0.2 cents profit on an output of $0.22 cents for materials. Her economy had no connection with the economics he taught, and he set out to remedy this state of affairs.[13]

Over the next decade, Yunus created the Grameen Bank, an institution which upended all banking conventions to lend money in tiny amounts to the most economically excluded people in Bangladesh – landless women. They had no collateral and were regarded as 'unbankable' from every point of view. His workers met potential clients in their homes, and peer groups of borrowers committed themselves to abide by Grameen's lending and repayment code. By 1998, Grameen had 12,000 employees, 1,112 branches, and 2,300,000 borrowers; $35 million went out in loans every month. Over 500 types of economic activity were listed in their annual report, including manufacture of cosmetics, toys, perfume, mosquito nets, candles, shoes, pickles, bread, clocks, umbrellas, spices, fire-crackers and soft drinks. The repayment rate was 98 per cent, to which Yunus compared the risible ten per cent recovery rate of the Bangladesh Industrial

Development Bank. Its propertied debtors endlessly defaulted on their loans, pleading a difficult industrial climate. Meanwhile illiterate, landless and secluded women had proved that, given a bank with which they could easily interact, as borrowers they represented almost no risk at all.

Yunus was not the only pioneer in micro-loan financing. Esther Ocloo of Ghana and Ela Bhatt of India – both of whom worked with market women in the informal economy – helped set up Women's World Banking in 1979. Like Yunus, they initially accepted soft loans from international bodies to recycle them in tiny amounts to customers; but the ultimate aim was self-sufficiency – dependence on people's own energy and resourcefulness. In the years since these organizations began, 31 million people, three-quarters of them women and two-thirds classified as the 'poorest of the poor', have received micro-loans in more than 40 countries.[14] The Grameen model has been exported to 58 other countries, including the US.

Small-scale entrepreneurship fuelled by small-scale loans has proved an alternative path to economic advancement for the poor – one that has immaculate capitalist credentials. The vital clue to its success is that the system operates within the economy of the customers, not the economy of the industrialized world that could never afford to service the tiny loans and mini-transactions. So bridges can be built between traditional and modern economies, but they require imagination and huge determination to buck the prevailing tide.

Harnessing technology

For others starting where people are and working with them to transform their economic productivity, the key input has not been to do with financial transaction, but with its partner in progress: technology.

One such pioneer is Rajendra Singh. In 1984 he visited Alwar district in the parched Indian state of Rajasthan. He found waterless villages and people migrating away to the towns in droves. At the suggestion of a village elder, Singh resurrected a traditional water-harvesting technology fallen into disuse. He built *johads* – small earthen embankments or 'check-dams' – in the beds of seasonal rivers to arrest rainwater during the monsoon.

Since then, the organization he formed, Tarun Bharat Sangh (TBS), has helped build 4,500 small dams and other rainwater harvesting structures. This has led to the regeneration of dried-up rivers and transformed the agricultural economy of 147 villages. Two-thirds were built without the help of an engineer, and at a ridiculously low cost compared to the concrete massifs favored by the planners. The water table has risen from a depth of 61 to 9 meters, and after successive years of drought, most *johads* contain water when everything else is dry. The *johads* represent an assertion by local people of ownership over their critical economic resources – land and water, and of their capacity to manage them without government help.

Singh's work is not unique. In other Indian drought-prone states – Gujarat, Maharashtra, Madhya Pradesh – water harvesting is also becoming a starting-point for community regeneration. The Centre for Science and Environment (CSE) based in Delhi has campaigned tirelessly to revive respect for traditional water harvesting techniques, document their effectiveness, and raise their profile where it counts.[15] But Rajendra Singh has been specially noticed. In 2001, he won a prestigious national prize, the Magsaysay Award. At the time of being garlanded, he was battling to prevent the irrigation authorities from tearing down a new 80-meter *johad* which they said was unsafe. It took a site occupation by villagers, and the intervention of prominent technical specialists to persuade the Chief Minister of Rajasthan to prevent the destruction. This was the 377th case taken out against Singh for building 'illegal' structures under laws left over from colonial times under the British *raj*.

There are many examples of 'appropriate' or low-tech solutions to development problems that are within the existing managerial and economic capacity of local communities. The difficulty is to attract investment and gain establishment interest. Local manufacture of water supply handpumps is one example of a community consumption and local industry fit. But unless some party – a non-governmental or aid organization or an enlightened entrepreneur – shoulders the initial research and development costs and takes the risks, efforts often run into the sand. The problem is that the standard-bearers of classic economic development have no interests at stake in helping local people assert their rights to their livelihood base. On the contrary: they often want to exploit that livelihood base for their own purposes, as did the British *raj*. So they either obstruct or stay away.

Building bridges

It would be unrealistic to expect that the expansion of the global marketplace can be stopped in its tracks. And for many of the workers employed in its local subsidiaries, what must be looked for is not an end to their jobs but more security, better pay and improved working conditions. But at the same time, it does not seem too much to ask that more attempts be made to build bridges from existing economies which macroeconomists ignore, to modern economic planning and banking institutions. At present, many local ways of life are being ground into dust or turned into a heritage museum marketed to tourists. This bridge-building requirement applies not only to rural economies based on natural resources but also to the informal trading, manufacturing and service economies of the urban poor.

There are many development commentators in the South who would echo Helena Norberg-Hodge's call for 'counter-development', a decentralized process that permits diversity, and builds on, rather than destroys, local systems. It has to be the case that there are other ways out of 'poverty' than for everyone to become card-carrying members of a high capital- and energy-intensive society – for which several more planetfuls of resources would anyway be required. Unfortunately, even while agreeing that globalization has damaged poor societies, few members of the development establishment seem able to think outside standard economic constructs and commit resources to approaches coming from elsewhere. They do not make the effort to understand other economies than their own. They think investment on a massive scale is needed, when at community level millions of very tiny investments, carefully and collectively planned, would be far better. If the investors cannot operate at that level, then you would think they could manage to operate at one or two rungs up. But they rarely even try on any significant scale.

Current proposals for adjusting the globalization process in favor of poor people amount to tinkering around the edges: reduce the exclusion of Southern commodities from Northern markets, focus aid more tightly, boost civil society and let the market do the rest. They fail to see that poor people in all their many manifestations – 'new' poor, 'old' poor, urban, rural, farming poor, trading poor, low-waged poor – will never have their problems solved by speeding up the extension of mainstream economic growth into their midst. Such proposals seem to assume there is no alternative to the economic and technological models that have served the North. Those who show that there is – Ela Bhatt, Mohammed Yunus, Rajendra Singh and others – are fêted and given platform-room at international meetings. Their critiques of what is happening in the name of development are vigorously applauded, but they do not lead to a revision of basic principles. Their ideas are appropriated but the lessons are only absorbed in a synthetic and peripheral way.

Somehow, if their poverty-reduction strategies are

larded with the right vocabulary – 'good governance' is the current flavor of the day – the experts seem to think that they have dealt with the biases, obstructionism and sheer lack of concern which disqualify so many groups of 'poor' from productive economic life. If more experts actually took the trouble to familiarize themselves with the realities of such people's lives, maybe they would be able to see how cosmetic much of this policy tinkering actually is. Then, perhaps, they might find ways to make useful links – useful from everyone's perspective – between multi-million investment packages and people whose resource base is vanishing from beneath their feet.

In the meantime, since economic growth was not a panacea, they have managed to accept that development does require up-front social investments. That is where we turn next.

1 'Aid packages ignore starving Afghans', Suzanne Goldenberg, *The Guardian*, 4 February 2002. **2** *Can anyone hear us?* Deepa Narayan, with Raj Patel, Kai Schafft, Anne Rademacher, Sarah Koch-Schulte, Book 1 of the *Voices of the Poor* study, Oxford University Press and the World Bank, 2000. **3** 'They only "hold pen"', Maggie Black, *New Internationalist* 336, July 2001. **4** *Human Development Report 1999,* UNDP/ Oxford University Press. **5** 'Quality and inequality' Zygmunt Bauman, in *The Moral Universe,* ed Tom Bentley and Daniel Steadman Jones, Demos, London, 2002. **6** See for example the UK Government White Paper of this title, DfID, 2001. **7** *The Poverty Curtain,* Mahbub ul Haq, Columbia University Press, 1976. **8** *The No-Nonsense Guide to Globalization,* Wayne Ellwood, *New Internationalist* and Verso, 2001. **9** *The Myth of Development*, Oswaldo de Riviero, Zed Books and others, 2001. **10** *Ancient Futures: Learning from Ladakh*, Helena Norberg-Hodge, Rider, 2000. **11** *Human Development Report 1999,* UNDP/Oxford University Press. **12** *Visions of the Future,* Robert Heilbroner, Oxford University Press, 1995. **13** *Banker to the Poor*, Mohamed Yunus with Alan Jolis, Aurum Press, 1998. **14** *State of the World 2002*, Worldwatch Institute, quoting papers from the NGO Microcredit Summit held in 2000. **15** '*Dying Wisdom'*, ed Anil Agarwal and Sunita Narain, *State of India's Environment Report* No 4, CSE, Delhi, 1997.

4 Social progress matters

Although the economic players have occupied development's commanding heights, those engaged in social progress eventually gained some recognition. That's the least they deserve. Most of the current wisdom comes from the social sphere, not the economic. Despite greater acknowledgement that development should focus on people's wellbeing, and not on national balance sheets, progress measured in terms of the human condition is still unsatisfactory.

WHEN ROBERT McNAMARA, then its president, persuaded the World Bank in 1973 to re-direct its policies towards the poorest 40 per cent of citizens in developing countries, a Rubicon was crossed. No longer was 'development' a purely economic concept, but it embraced social purpose too. Those who had been laboring in the social vineyard for nearly two decades were delighted that their activities had belatedly won some heavyweight credibility.

It was not actually news to the social players – governmental, international, and non-governmental organizations (NGOs) – that they were contributing to development. Since the 1950s, the World Health Organization (WHO) and the UN Children's Fund (UNICEF) had supported mass onslaughts against epidemic disease throughout the developing world[1]. This was the 'new look' in public health, made possible by post-War advances in medical science: vaccines, penicillin, mass DDT spraying against the malarial mosquito. The latter ultimately failed, but malaria was dramatically reduced for a time: in India, from 100 million cases a year to 80,000. The eradication of smallpox succeeded: the last case was in Somalia in 1977. The expense of the campaigns was justified by the economic productivity better health would unleash. They had a remarkable effect in saving lives and reducing misery, especially in Asia, where their demographic impact was also quickest to raise concern.

The disease campaigns were international public health's brand leader but not its only pursuit. The predominant motif of underdevelopment was the hungry child, and considerable resources were spent tackling malnutrition. At the time it was believed that the main culprit was insufficient protein in the diet of young children. 'Protein malnutrition' was seen as an epidemic 'disease', susceptible to treatment by a dietary medicine. So in the heyday of belief in technology's supernatural powers, scientists set out to grind oilseeds, peanuts, soy and fish and create foodstuffs to solve the 'protein crisis'. But processed foods were beyond the financial reach of poor people. Eventually it transpired that protein was not the demon of malnutrition: calories were just as important. The idea of a worldwide 'protein gap' was dismissed as a myth.

Child nutrition re-emerged on the international agenda with the campaign to control the marketing of infant formula in developing countries. The damage to infant health was a bellwether of what could happen when large corporations sought to penetrate their wares into societies that lacked the knowledge or means to use them properly. The campaign peaked in the 1980s, with WHO and UNICEF ranged with the NGOs and activists against the companies and their political allies. It led to an international program of support to breast-feeding. Apart from attention to deficiencies of micronutrients such as Vitamin A and iodine, nutrition issues have since been subsumed under the heading of 'food insecurity'. An inadequate diet, after all, is less the product of dietary ignorance or specific deficiency than lack of a secure hold on the means to a livelihood. 'Entitlement' to a supply of food, as the Nobel Laureate economist Amartya Sen famously argued, is the point.[2]

A patchy record

We could run the gamut of activity in the social sectors

during the early decades of development and find that there were as many mistakes as glowing improvements. Rural water supplies? A litany of broken-down pumps and no-one to mend them. Contraception? Unwanted, because the family planning strategy then applied by pre-industrial societies was maximization of family size to provide security in old age. NGOs that took up development similarly found that their expectations were naive. Ways of doing things that had served people well for generations were not instantly abandoned because strangers appeared in their midst, extolling the virtues of new seeds, foods or pills.

It was not surprising that the record in the social sphere was patchy. In rural areas – and in poor urban areas as these multiplied – the service network was embryonic. In much of Africa it was non-existent. Healthcare, schooling, welfare, where they were available, were provided by missionaries. These operated in small, scattered oases, for a surrounding clientele. The colonizing powers had focused on producing a handful of educated people to serve the governing, professional and commercial élite. For the rest, tilling the soil and digging the mines required little formal learning. Healthcare and other social amenities were concentrated exclusively in principal towns. So the development of national social networks was a truly daunting proposition. Given the difficulties, the advances achieved in education, life expectancy and disease reduction in the early development decades were remarkable even if they were modest.

When the big-league players began to intervene in the social sphere, the formula they came up with was that the various sectoral activities should be 'integrated' – fitted together so that they reinforced each other. Roads, clinics, water supplies, transport, communications, schools, would be introduced *en masse* in a given district. The problem with these plans was that integration rarely extended beyond them. Meetings might take place between national ministries, but out

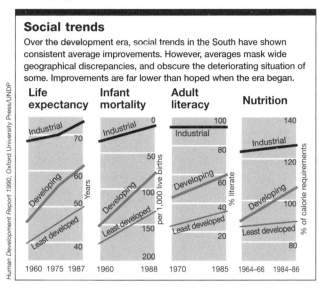

Human Development Report 1990, Oxford University Press/UNDP

Social trends

Over the development era, social trends in the South have shown consistent average improvements. However, averages mask wide geographical discrepancies, and obscure the deteriorating situation of some. Improvements are far lower than hoped when the era began.

in 'the field' synchronized inputs to bring about socio-economic transformation were an illusion. People might arrive one day and build something; different people might arrive some months later and build something else. All this happened without reference to local people. Whether it benefited them was hit or miss – there was nothing resembling appropriate planning according to their needs or wishes.

The case was somewhat different for NGOs. Partly because the social improvers were bit-players in financial terms for whom 'small' was not only beautiful but the only option, those engaged in improving the condition of people at the end of the road managed to absorb 'lessons learned' relatively early. Since the test of what they were doing was whether people's wellbeing actually improved, not what showed up in the latest financial or economic data, they had a reality check. They saw what worked or did not. The best of them adjusted – or tried to.

Almost all the radical thinking about development

and how it might work for poor people has come from the social players and most of it has been pioneered by local people – including incomers and some localized expatriates – with or without small amounts of external support. The need for genuine alternatives to mainstream models did not pass them by, nor was it dismissed as romantic conservatism or left-wing dissent.

Doings things differently: health...

If the export of Western models failed to benefit poor people economically, the same was true in the social sphere. Where 90 per cent of a country's health budget was spent on a handful of high-tech hospitals dispensing medical care for the few, the health of 90 per cent of the country's population was ignored.

The disease campaigns did involve public health outreach. But they were all run by special teams that traveled to the periphery and then disappeared back to town. It became obvious that a progressive extension of standard medical services would take generations. Doctors did not want to serve in rural areas where facilities were inadequate, drugs non-existent, and the caseload of coughs, fevers and diarrheal infections beneath the dignity of their professional qualifications. Radical new thinking from the ground up was required if healthcare was to be provided for all.

Examples of alternative models were available. In the 1970s, China's 'barefoot doctors' had been trained to treat symptoms of common diseases, provide health education and refer cases they could not manage to clinics and hospitals, which could. A number of successful experiments were also undertaken by dedicated professionals in Bangladesh, Tanzania, Guatemala and elsewhere along similar decentralized lines. Many set out to train volunteers living in the community to perform basic health-related tasks. Their cumulated experience became the basis for WHO's adoption in 1978 of a strategy for 'primary healthcare' whereby village-based workers would help communities achieve 'health for all'.

The ideology of 'health by the people' was, at its extreme, very radical: some saw the democratization and demedicalization of healthcare as ends in themselves. Certainly, they represented an ideological attack on Westernized approaches and a commitment to supporting people's own abilities to define and meet their needs.

...and education

There was a similarly radical overhaul of educational thinking. In the early days of the development mission, the appetite for learning and need for personnel in all branches of the nation-building project meant that education was one of the largest growth industries in developing countries, absorbing 15-25 per cent of budgets. But the rate of growth could not be sustained, even as age cohorts swelled and extra places were needed. Critics also pointed to the irrelevance of curricula to the realities of life most students could expect and the way it was geared to providing a chosen few with white-collar jobs and frustration for the rest.

The increase in school-goers was, moreover, less a cause for celebration than it seemed. Philip Coombs, a leading analyst, wrote: 'The figures are silent about the dark side. They do not reveal the vast social waste and the human tragedy in the high rate of dropouts and failures. They hide the large number of costly "repeaters". They say nothing about the nature, quality and usefulness of the education received.' So disenchanted were some reformers that they advocated the removal of schools altogether. The Brazilian educator Paulo Freire was sent into exile for stating that the existing system was an instrument for reinforcing economic, social and political oppression.

Education, therefore, also experienced its radical phase, with 'barefoot' teachers, reintroduction of local languages as the medium of instruction, nonformal programs for women who had never gone to school and children who had 'dropped out'.

Increased productivity required that people – especially women – in semi-subsistence economies had a basic educational grounding and were open to change: even the World Bank agreed with that.

These ideas, informed by a range of experiences in the South, came together in the 'basic services strategy', an approach developed in the late 1970s combining 'integrated' and 'barefoot'. Basic services envisaged the extension to communities of a complementary package – primary healthcare, water supply, sanitation, nutrition, income-generation for women – through the agency of community-based workers. Not only would this help spread services to the periphery, it would also mean that what was done would have to respond to the real needs and desires of communities, and that they would be involved. The authorities' job would be to supervise, co-ordinate, provide technical back up and adjust inputs appropriately.

The promise of the 'basic services strategy' was higher than its yield: many developing country governments resisted radically restructuring services towards their more deprived populations. And then came the nightmare of 'structural adjustment' which thoroughly derailed social spending. Nonetheless, the impulse to design services so as to reach far-flung communities did have lasting effect. So did the realization that people in 'poor' societies could be agents of change in their own lives and were not merely passive victims of hunger, ill-health and other 'poverty' characteristics as labeled and described by others.

A new focus on software

Thus the upending of Western models for social advance provided the laboratory from which emerged today's development tenets: 'participatory', 'decentralized', 'empowering', 'knowledge transfer' and the rest. This was the 'how' – the software ingredients which knocked from their pedestal the all-powerful hardware ingredients and their technical overlords –

engineers, planners and scientists. The new emphasis on processes, their stimulation and their management, was a useful corrective to the old idea that development was all about buildings, installations and technological devices. But it also helped to introduce a degree of incoherence. If what a community wanted were a year-round water supply, a functioning village dispensary and a school with teachers, books, desks and pencils, it was hard for them to appreciate that a 'knowledge transfer' or 'attitudinal change' would do the trick. Tangible benefits were also needed, and sometimes the pendulum swung too far in the software direction.

However, the alternative approaches were better

The HIV crisis

The HIV/AIDS pandemic emerged in the 1990s. Since women and men in the prime of economic life are mainly affected, the infection devastates household economies and leaves children and the elderly without means of support. Africa has suffered disastrously, containing 70 per cent of those infected and 90 per cent of AIDS orphans. Of the five million new infections in 2000, 50 per cent were among young people aged 15-24, with girls and women especially vulnerable. In the worst affected areas, the under-five mortality rate is expected to double by 2010.

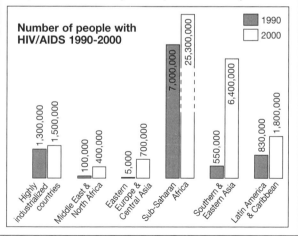

Number of people with HIV/AIDS 1990-2000

geared to the actual needs of communities. The diverse nature of 'the poor' became more visible: poverty was not a uniform phenomenon and its victims could not all be lumped into one conceptual basket. The particular predicaments of women were increasingly recognized; children as a sub-group also become more noticed as an outcome of social disintegration and family breakdown. Concern was also focused on those threatened with indigence because of war or famine displacement, disability, family disaster, or chronic illness including HIV/AIDS.

The specific circumstances of any population group, and of target groups within it, were accommodated in activities in which they were to participate. The master plan approach gave ground to the plan developed on site and tried out on a small scale before going into overdrive.

In the 1990s, the attention given to the software of development led to a greater emphasis on education, and to the critical state into which schooling had descended. Since 1980, the proportion of school-going 6-11 year olds had fallen in many countries, and in Africa, educational expenditure per person had more than halved. Yet study after study showed that almost every form of social improvement – from increased farming productivity to family planning take-up, lowered child mortality to increased employment – depended on the amount and quality of education people, especially women, received. In 1990, an international conference on education confirmed the right of every person in the world to a basic package of knowledge and skills, and launched an initiative to achieve 'Education for All'. This included universal primary education and major reductions in adult illiteracy through non-formal programs for girls, out-of-school and street children, ethnic and indigenous groups.

During this period, the frustration felt by many social development organizations began to express itself in another form of software: 'advocacy'. NGOs and international bodies commissioned their own research, analyzed data and began to issue reports calling for policy change in every imaginable area. This generated prescriptions by the score and contributed to 'the policy debate'. But without another essential piece of software in place – the political and administrative infrastructure to deliver policy on the ground – questions remained about what, in real terms, the mounting frenzy of advocacy could achieve.

Links with economic concerns

One of the most conspicuous features of social programs was that they quickly began to embrace economic and livelihood issues. Take women as an example. Originally, women were seen purely as recipients of welfare. But they are key providers to the household and without efforts to help them generate income, family wellbeing could not improve. Whether by food production, petty manufacture or trading, or by assuring them a role in decision-making, women needed to exert more control in the economic sphere for there to be social impacts – improved child health and nutrition, higher enrolment for children in school – from increased productivity.

As the women's movement gathered pace, it exposed the ways in which development had discriminated against women, opening up educational and employment opportunity to men, and leaving women stranded in menial roles – a phenomenon known as 'the feminization of poverty'. In some countries, over 90 per cent of women working outside agriculture are in the informal sector.[3] Many more are entering it, not as an act of liberated choice, but because they desperately need some cash. Women also provided all social and healthcare, either in their family roles or as 'community workers' in basic services. Because women in developing countries fought for it, attention to gender roles and affirmative action to improve women's status became an accepted norm in development policy.

In other social programs, economic components kept creeping in. This often began with the need to provide for local maintenance of a community installation – a water pump, for example. Or to provide stipends for community workers. Few efforts to extend services entirely by the state – even where the state was willing – worked well; facilities often broke down or remained unused. Where communities paid for the teacher's house or the new washing place, services were better grounded, better 'owned' and used. Thus many social schemes relied on local systems of community levy, 'revolving funds', or subsidized sale of home improvements to multiply their impact and establish their activities in the social mainstream. The willingness of people to pay for sanitary facilities, daycare centers, or a basketball court to keep their children out of trouble, was an indication of their interest. And if the economics worked, and the social improvement fitted their consumer reality – tin roofs in East Africa, or tubewells in Bangladesh, for example – it entered their own economy and generated its own mini-industry and local jobs. Thus the social development actors did find ways to build bridges between traditional economies and the local, semi-formal, market.

Demand and willingness to pay

The downside of the social actors' success in the economic sphere is that the economists have latched on to 'willingness to pay' as an indication of market demand's supremacy even in the social sphere, even among people with very few cash resources. They talk of 'full cost recovery' and advocate cuts in subsidies at the earliest opportunity, even when it is clear that many services cannot reach the periphery without subsidies, nor were they ever expected to do so in the industrialized world.

In many Southern settings, the provision of services is already skewed by the realities of social hierarchy, wealth and political influence. They are subsidized in favor of the élite; it seems grossly unjust therefore to make people who are much worse off and suffering discrimination pay fully for them. Yet this is the cornerstone of the World Bank's poverty reduction strategies – its latest display of commitment to the idea that social investments matter. Yes, they matter, but they will have to be paid for. This applies to healthcare, schooling, water and sanitation. Ghana, held up as a textbook case of the efficacy of the IMF/World Bank strategy for economic recovery, expects even the poorest pregnant mother to pay for her hospital delivery, and even a bucket of water from a standpipe carries user-charges.[4] People's 'willingness to pay' for things they cannot do without has been interpreted as an indication of their 'demand' – and become a stick with which to beat them.

Meanwhile, if there is evidence of a demand for services within a traditional economic framework, they will be commercialized by the advocates of market economics. People in traditional occupations are cut out – water sellers, waste-collectors, street cleaners, snack-food makers, for example. The prices of the new goods and services invariably end up higher than those of the traditional providers they displace. 'Efficiency' requires involvement from the modern economy with its superior technology and know-how; but the higher costs of its apparatus and profits have to be passed down. Not only are services provided by commercial water and fuel companies unaffordable for those in low-income groups but they destroy the invisible economies on which informal systems were based. Governments that have been corrupt and inefficient in service delivery cannot be expected to regulate the private sector effectively, nor do they have any incentive to do so. And so the carousel of exclusion goes round.

Social improvement – or destruction?

Some critics blame the social improvers almost as vehemently as the economic planners for the destruction of traditional lifestyles brought about by 'progress'. But the case is harder to make. Many of the cultural practices they try to erode – female genital mutilation, for example – are indefensible, and are opposed in the societies concerned. Safer childbirth is important; over half a million women still die every year from complications in pregnancy and during delivery. Some beliefs and practices surrounding cleanliness and the routes of all kinds of infectious diseases could do with displacement by scientific fact. Most people support decent education, even for girls. But in certain cases, the iniquitous intrusion of consumerism and modern technology into places where ancient ideas hold sway tends to make them more pernicious. The availability of cheap ultrasound tests to determine the sex of an unborn child is one example: this can lead to the abortion of unwanted girls, and is being spread by unscrupulous medical practitioners throughout the Indian sub-continent.

The better social development practitioners build bridges to ease the transition from old ways to new and, by providing information and education, try to enable people and communities make informed choices about what they want to do. In other cases social activists hold the line against the forces of displacement. Today, many of those committed to social improvement find that their principal occupation is to react to the misery inflicted on already disadvantaged groups by the purveyors of the capitalist mode of economic development. This is not a romantic pre-occupation with the past, but a confrontation over first principles which is becoming uglier by the day.

Re-shaping the development mission

In 1990, the UN Development Program (UNDP) published the first of its annual *Human Development Reports.* This was an initiative of Mahbub ul Haq, previously a Minister of Finance in Pakistan, who persuaded UNDP to give his project house room and a budget. The report opened as follows: 'The real wealth of a nation is its people. And the purpose of development is to create an enabling environment for people to enjoy long, healthy and creative lives. This simple but powerful truth is too often forgotten in the pursuit of material and financial wealth.'

Nearly two decades had passed since social development first received an international seal of approval. But the main players had gone on measuring development by the same economic criteria: growth in GNP per capita, which simply divides the national cake by the number of inhabitants, indicating nothing about their state of wellbeing. In spite of growing interest in social concerns, social indicators – life expectancy, infant mortality, illiteracy and malnutrition – were still seen as adjuncts to the main game of sum national economic advance. Haq was determined to place what

The Human Development Index (HDI)

In 1990, the first annual UN Human Development Report introduced the Human Development Index (HDI). To show countries' real level of development, two social indicators – life expectancy and adult literacy – were combined with national income in a composite measure of 'human development'. The HDI was crude and its methodology has since been endlessly refined. But the central point is important: a country's wealth is a limited guide to its citizens' state of personal and collective wellbeing, In the chart, see how Vietnam, with an income of under $2,000 per capita, ranks high on the HDI scale, alongside South Africa whose income is considerably larger. However Guinea, with about the same income as Vietnam and Pakistan, has a much lower HDI ranking of 0.397.

No automatic link between income and human development

*PPP = Purchasing power parity rates of exchange

Human Development Report 2001, Oxford University Press/UNDP development was doing to humanity on center stage.

The 'human development' thesis was that wide-ranging analysis of development experience taught lessons about investment in people that could be widely implemented in favor of social advance. These lessons applied in countries as divergent as Cuba and Taiwan, Mexico and Sri Lanka, Egypt and Vietnam. Some countries had managed to achieve all but 'developed' status according to such criteria as low infant mortality, high literacy and strong service coverage, but were still poor by any application of standard economic criteria. The Human Development Report proposed that a composite 'human development index' would give a more realistic picture of the state of development in a given country.

The idea was to prompt those with reasonable incomes but weak social performance to reorient policies and resources so that economic success could be transformed into human wellbeing. The ranking of countries against the index caused controversy, not least among those countries that performed poorly. But in many quarters the idea was widely applauded. The annual *Human Development Reports* have since made an important contribution to the development debate, internationally and within countries of the South. The promotion of social components as critical to development was part of a wider effort during the 1990s to help push the condition of humanity, especially its poorer members, nearer to the center of international concern.

Social development goals

The idea of measuring development by means of social indicators was not new, but it had taken time to gain an imprimatur from a key international gate-keeper. In 1976, the think tank known as the Club of Rome published a report entitled 'Reshaping the International Order', calling for the setting of global targets on infant mortality, life expectancy, literacy and lowered birth rate to be reached by 2000.

In the early 1980s, UNICEF's Executive Director, James Grant, elevated reduced infant mortality to pole position in the organization's mission, and set out to generate political and popular momentum behind 'child survival'. Grant was the first head of an international development organization to attempt to build an international alliance around time-bound social goals. He was very aware that, without an early success, the strategy would flounder. UNICEF's initial focus was on universal childhood immunization. The drive was highly successful: by enlisting presidents and influential partners in the countries concerned, many achieved immunization rates of 75 per cent by 1990.

At the 1990 World Summit for Children – an event masterminded by Grant – a number of global social goals were internationally accepted. These included reductions by 2000 in infant and young child mortality; maternal mortality, child malnutrition and illiteracy; universal access to safe water and sanitation and to primary education. In a number of countries, national programs of action were developed. Although it took time to gain more than rhetorical commitment to this new version of the development mission, the idea of focusing on key social indicators as manifestations of poverty to be directly addressed was promoted throughout the 1990s at UN Summits and Conferences. In 1996, the club of donor countries reconfirmed these

---

The millennial goals

♦ Reduce by 50 per cent the share of the world's people living in extreme poverty, suffering from hunger and lacking access to clean drinking water

♦ Reduce maternal mortality by 75 per cent

♦ Reduce mortality rates for children under five by 66 per cent

♦ Achieve universal primary education and gender equality in access to education

♦ Halt, then reverse, the spread of HIV/AIDS, malaria and other major diseases. ■

Human Development Report 2001, OUP/UNDP

targets, now with deadlines of 2015; the UN Millennium Summit in 2000 conferred the final seal of international approval. In theory at least, a new socially oriented push against poverty was underway.

What is the record?

In time for the new millennium, the development mission thus received a long overdue facelift to try to ensure that the human improvement it was always intended to secure would not be left to happen coincidentally as a product of economic advance, but was placed at its heart. However, for all the target-setting, results in most areas are disappointing.

The *Human Development Report* consistently draws attention to the improvements of the past 50 years and the positive trends in many areas – the 'cup half-full' rather than 'half-empty' approach. And – except in sub-Saharan Africa – life expectancy at birth does continue to rise, infant mortality is tending to drop, and the rate of school enrolment is rising. But the plain truth is that, in absolute terms, the numbers have shown little improvement, and within certain countries and regions, especially in Africa, the situation of the poorest is getting worse.

Between 1990 and 2000, the reduction in the death rate of children under five only improved on average by 11 per cent, not by the one-third target set.[5] In 1990, 100 million school-age children never went to school; by 2000, the number had increased to 120 million. Those without enough to eat decreased from 841 million in 1990-1992 to 792 million in 1996-98; nowhere near the number needed to meet the target reduction of 50 per cent by 2015.[6] Some supporting targets – the reduction by half of child deaths from diarrheal infections – were on track. But the major goals for 2015 in health, nutritional and educational contexts cannot possibly be reached. That they have been internationally agreed means that they can be used to exert leverage to attempt fulfillment. In practice, the record has been disappointing.

At the 1994 World Social Summit, a 20/20 compact was proposed whereby developing countries would commit 20 per cent of their public expenditures to the provision of basic social services, and donor countries would similarly commit 20 per cent of their aid expenditures. NGOs proposed that the share of social sector spending be 50 per cent, including basic services and support to micro-credit and income-generation. Governments agreed to 20/20, on a voluntary basis. But in 2000, UNICEF estimated that developing countries committed only 12-14 per cent of their expenditures to basic services, and that 15 per cent of official development aid flows went on their spread. In its review of progress over the 1990s, UNICEF cryptically commented that many developing countries had not been able to learn the lessons of flawed and inadequate past social policies. 'For the most part', stated the report, 'they did not manage to focus their programs and resources on the most disadvantaged children and families, nor did they alter their policies to take account of the experience of previous decades.'

In sub-Saharan Africa, where the picture is worst, the impacts of pervasive conflict, HIV/AIDS and the continuing burden of debt combine to make social progress ever more elusive. In the most badly hit countries, life expectancy is dropping and child mortality soaring. A report from Oxfam – one of a number of international NGOs to call for governments to deliver on their commitment to 'Education for All' – describes how parents in the three countries they researched (Ghana, Tanzania and Zambia) – say that education charges frequently force them to make impossible choices: whether to buy basic medicines or keep their children in school.[7]

Meanwhile, WHO and UNICEF have entered deals with the pharmaceutical industry, which is looking to play a part in provision of HIV/AIDS treatments, malarial control and vaccine provision. There is anxiety that public-private partnership is now creeping into the social sphere and that its pursuit of profits and profit margins will reinforce the exclusion from which so many already suffer, rendering unaffordable to those in lower income groups drugs, treatments, condoms, mosquito nets, and all manner of items.

For many reasons – and they include failures of commitment on every side – the extension of affordable basic services is not going forward with anything like the momentum needed. Nor are livelihood schemes to assure people a basic 'entitlement' – the means either to grow or to buy enough food for their families to eat and meet other essentials. Meanwhile, the volume of social stress continues to rise. Displaced families; those decimated by HIV/AIDS; those dependent on a sole woman earner whose hold on any form of income is insecure at best; landless families, urban poor families; families with working children, children on their own. These constitute the ten or 20 per cent, sometimes 50 per cent, of those whom services do not reach or who cannot afford to use them. Even if there have been major social gains in global terms over the era of development, the proportions of those unreached represent very sizeable numbers. Without radical policy change their outlook can only get worse.

One important ingredient of such policy change is the protection of the natural environment on which so many livelihoods depend. 'Sustainability' is the next direction in which to explore the development conundrum.

1 *The Children and the Nations,* Maggie Black, Macmillan and UNICEF, 1987; and *Children First*, Oxford University Press and UNICEF, 1996. **2** *Poverty and famines: An essay on entitlement and deprivation,* Amartya Sen, Clarendon Press, 1984. **3** *The World's Women, Trends and Statistics,* United Nations, 2000. **4** 'Cash and carry misery in Ghana', John Kampfner, *The Guardian*, February 8 2002. **5** *We the Children,* Report by the UN Secretary-General on progress since the World Summit for Children, UNICEF 2001. **6** *The State of Food Insecurity in the World*, FAO, 1999. **7** *Education Charges: A Tax on Human Development,* Oxfam Policy Paper, 2001.

5 Enter 'sustainability'

Environmental concerns were first coupled to development in the early 1970s, but not until the 1987 Brundtland Report came up with the concept of 'sustainable development' were they definitively linked. The idea of eco-friendly socio-economic advance was very appealing. The 1992 Earth Summit put the concept on the map and since then the word 'sustainable' has been applied to everything done in development's name. But to what avail? The global commons of air, water, fuel, biodiversity continue to be threatened.

IN 1983, THE UN Secretary-General invited Norwegian prime minister Gro Harlem Brundtland to chair a World Commission on Environment and Development. Concern about the acute pressure of population growth, modern technology and consumer demand on the planetary fabric had been smoldering away since the 1970s. Now a new generation of environmental worries – species loss, global warming, deforestation, toxic wastes – had begun to capture scientific and popular attention. The world's natural resources were being rapidly depleted, often in the name of development, but the poverty this development was supposed to correct was as widespread as ever.

Ever since the global environment first became a matter of international concern in the late 1960s, a few committed publicists for development such as the economist Barbara Ward had linked its plunder with world poverty.[1] Waste, pollution, nuclear proliferation and over-consumption of the earth's natural wealth were counterpoised with humanity's unwillingness to do much for people living in poverty. But her synthesis of environmental and development issues was then unusual. More attention was captured by dire prognostications of planetary disaster. Two of the most influential were *Limits to Growth* by the Club of Rome and *Blueprint for Survival* by the UK journal *The Ecologist*, both published in 1972. These alarm calls about the rapid exhaustion of resources sent shockwaves around the world. Their computer-modeled rates of depletion turned out to be exaggerated, but they exerted a powerful force on the human conscience and prompted calls for 'back to nature' restraint.

However, there was a problem with much of this analysis of environmental stress: it was biased against poor countries. Their extraordinary fertility was blamed for precipitating a global population crisis. Demographic trends had gone mad. Plummeting death rates – for which the mass disease campaigns were held responsible – had not been accompanied by corresponding declines in birth rates.

Populations had soared in the poorer parts of the globe, especially in Asia and Africa, with typical growth rates of over two per cent a year.[2] The effect of this over time was startling. First, the population rapidly became younger, with up to half under the age of 15. Secondly, the rate of growth was exponential: 50 per cent more citizens in 16 years, double the number in 25. World population had taken 120 years to grow from one to two billion people but just 35 years to reach three billion around 1960. The intervals to each successive billion would shorten dramatically.

When first observed, this unprecedented phenomenon provoked a Malthusian panic. How would a planet bursting at the seams manage to feed, shelter and provide for all these people? The spectacle arose of humankind reproducing itself at such a pace as to devour the world's supply of natural resources within a few generations. Without a drastic curtailment of fertility, all prospects of development would lag further behind. No resource base could be expected to produce improvements in quality of life for populations that doubled themselves in less than a generation.

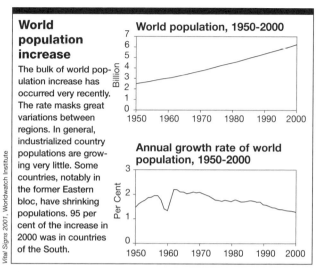

World population increase

The bulk of world population increase has occurred very recently. The rate masks great variations between regions. In general, industrialized country populations are growing very little. Some countries, notably in the former Eastern bloc, have shrinking populations. 95 per cent of the increase in 2000 was in countries of the South.

World population, 1950-2000

Annual growth rate of world population, 1950-2000

Vital Signs 2001, Worldwatch Institute

Curbing population growth

Certain countries – those that were populous and already densely settled such as India and China – took this constraint to socio-economic progress very seriously. There was no time to wait for the 'demographic transition' to lower fertility that accompanied prosperity: in the industrialized world this had taken at least a generation. China imposed its one-child policy. India introduced a draconian measure of enforced sterilization in the 1970s, but had to withdraw it in the face of social and political upheaval. Elsewhere, the call for population control fell largely on deaf ears. Catholic countries were opposed. In Africa, a larger population was thought necessary for nation-building, and strictures to reduce fertility with contraceptives was seen as cultural imperialism, distasteful and racist.

'Population control' eventually became an anathema. The unwelcome attempts to tie tubes, fit loops and get women to swallow pills all over the developing world created a backlash – assisted by the Vatican. Most people in non-industrial societies needed large families to provide labor and assure security in old age. Only when families moved to cramped living-quarters in town – as many more were doing – and became dependent on cash did children become an economic burden. The 'demographic transition' gradually started almost everywhere. By century's end the overall growth rate had slowed to 1.2 per cent. But in the poorest groups in the poorest countries, fertility remained almost as high as ever.

Since the late 1980s, many family planning programs have been absorbed into reproductive healthcare and education and opportunities for women promoted as a less controversial route to fertility reduction. Despite the impact of Northern consumption, the inescapable fact remains that population growth continues to exert huge pressures on the natural resource base, and on the increasingly stretched urban fabric of most countries in the South. World population reached five billion in 1987 and six billion in 1999. Dire predictions continue to be made of what will happen when there are 12 billion people on earth, but they do not cause the stir they used to.

Planetary threats

There is a simple reason. By the time the Brundtland Commission delivered its report on *Our Common Future* in 1987, population growth was no longer seen as the major threat to the harmony of the planet. Almost all population growth was among poorer people. And it was not they who were consuming the earth's supply of fossil fuels, warming the globe with their carbon emissions, depleting its ozone layer with their CFCs, poisoning soil and water with their chemicals, or wreaking ecological havoc with their oil spills. In fact, their consumption of the world's resources was minute compared to that of the industrialized world.

Brundtland declared that poverty in the developing world was less cause than effect of contemporary environmental degradation, the outcome of insensitive

The development gap

The chart shows the annual impact of 1,000 people in a developed and a developing country.

	In Germany		In a developing country	
Energy consumption (TJ)	158		22	(Egypt)
Greenhouse gases (t)	13,700		1,300	(Egypt)
Ozone depleting substances (kg)	450		16	(Philippines)
Roads (km)	8		0.7	(Egypt)
Freight transports (tkm)	4,391,000		776,000	(Egypt)
Passenger travel (pkm)	9,126,000		904,000	(Egypt)
Cars	443		6	(Philippines)
Aluminum consumption (t)	28		2	(Argentina)
Cement consumption (t)	413		56	(Philippines)
Steel consumption (t)	655		5	(Philippines)
Solid waste (t)	400		ca.120	(Philippines)
Hazardous waste (t)	187		ca. 2	(Philippines)

TJ = Tera Joule (1×10^{12} joules)   t = tons
tkm = ton kilometers   pkm = passenger kilometers

Sharing the World, Wuppertal Institute

technology transfer that pauperized people and natural systems. If all the world's people were to live like North Americans, a planet four times as large would be needed. Only 'sustainable' development could blend the fulfillment of human needs with the protection of air, soil, water and all forms of life – from which, ultimately, planetary stability was inseparable.

Thus the concept of 'sustainable development' was launched: social and economic advance to assure human beings a healthy and productive life, but one that did not jeopardize the right of coming generations to their own slice of the world's pie. Sustainable development was a big new idea. It brought environmentalism into poverty reduction and poverty reduction into environmentalism in a neat and simple formula. And the Brundtland Report attracted huge attention. It led on to the Earth Summit – the UN Conference on Environment and Development – at Rio de Janeiro in 1992, and to the formulation of *Agenda 21*, an internationally accepted 'blueprint for survival' of its day. The word 'sustainable' was absorbed into the development lexicon and has since been flogged, for everything from 'environmentally sensitive' to 'respect for indigenous ways of doing things' to 'affordable over the longer term'.

So what is the reality? Is sustainable development practicable, and if so, can it help the poor?

South versus North

When the first UN conference on the global environment was convened in Stockholm in 1972, the agenda was dictated by the West. There was resentment from the developing world: a regime of international ecological regulation – not in place during Western industrialization – would deny them a 'developed' future. Blocks on resource use would fix the world in permanent inequality between haves and have-nots.

Unlike 'development', which has always been perceived as exclusive to the South, environmental issues stretch all the way up from inside and outside anybody's door – be it in a suburban street, a rainforest clearing, or a stretch of African savanna – to the global commons of the biosphere. What everyone does affects 'the environment', and everyone else.

The US, with five per cent of the world's population, consumes 25 per cent of the world's yearly consumption of fossil fuels, and emits 20 per cent of its greenhouse gases. But the effects don't confront Americans daily on their doorsteps – on the contrary, there is no immediate sense of damage to the ecosystem. But the brunt of sea level change from global warming will be borne by people who live on delta plains in densely populated countries in Asia and Africa. A one-meter rise would displace four million coastal inhabitants in Nigeria, ten million in Vietnam and 15-20 million in Bangladesh.[3]

Here is a set of issues that imbue the cliché about living in an interdependent global village with real meaning. That does not necessarily make it easier to create a common sense of purpose between North and

South. Growth-led industrialization and trade is still the favored path to development of many countries set on becoming card-carrying members of the modern world, and they still raise the objections they raised in 1972. They do not want inhibiting and expensive environmental regulatory regimes – unless the industrialized world is willing to pay for them. The sum suggested in *Agenda 21* for this purpose was $125 billion – more than twice what is currently spent on aid.

Northern lack of restraint

Meanwhile the lack of willingness from the North, particularly the US, to regulate its own energy consumption, does little to encourage Southern governments to take resource conservation seriously. President George W Bush's unwillingness to sign the Kyoto agreement to cut greenhouse gas emissions does not help. In vain is it pointed out, even by their own experts, that since 90 per cent of population growth will take place in their countries, they will need to take a different path to progress from that trodden by the North if their industrializing environment is to remain habitable. Already, pollution, water and power shortages and traffic congestion beset Asia, Africa and Latin America. Jakarta and Shanghai suffer the world's worst air pollution. Traffic regularly grinds Lagos, Bangkok and Mumbai (Bombay) into gridlock.

However, there has been one important change in the South since the 1970s: a spectacular growth in grassroots movements devoted to environmental issues. Many of these have found common purpose with Northern counterparts at the international level. They network via the web and use joint leverage against international investment in large-scale power, water or agribusiness projects, or against such export sales as paper products from the destruction of tropical forests. Southern campaigns run the gamut from anti-dam movements to fisheries protection and freedom from genetically modified (GM) foods. Some are concerned with air quality from vehicle pollution, water-profligacy, or consumer waste. Many mind less about what is happening to the planet than about matters of life and death, here and now. Millions of people in the South, especially indigenous groups, are fighting to preserve the habitat they need to survive. For them, 'sustainability' is deadly serious.

The 1992 Earth Summit provided an important platform for the expression of activist concern from both North and South. The participation of NGOs in the preparation of *Agenda 21*, and in the Summit itself, showed a new legitimacy for citizen groups. This marked the moment at which the development mission as a campaign against world poverty became subsumed into the campaign for the environment under the 'sustainability' logo. The poverty of millions of people no longer had the power on its own to ignite worldwide fervor against the doctrine of unfettered growth. Whereas what this was doing to the natural world – to the climate, forests, soils, water resources, fish stocks, oceans, species, and to ecological integrity – became a universal banner under which activism in all parts of the world intensified.

Campaigns became specific and treated social and environmental aspects in tandem. No longer were the conservation of nature and the pursuit of humanity's wellbeing seen as mutually antagonistic. 'Sustainability' put them in bed together and gave impoverished societies a new platform and voice.

A green leap forward

What did the shift of focus achieve? The Earth Summit with its bevy of environmental conventions – on climate change, biodiversity, desertification, organic pollutants – was seen as a great green leap forward. The world entered a more environmentally conscious age and less polluting and energy-guzzling adaptations of everything from car exhausts, to refrigerators, to heating systems, flourished. Alternative energy via wind farms and solar panels has arrived. 'Ecological' is no longer a freak word but respectably mainstream: the first international conference on ecological sanitation – water-free toilets and recycled excreta – took place in China at the end of 2001.

In theory at least, all large projects now have to go through social and environmental hoops and clearance procedures. Where international investors are faced by the realities of what their investments will do, and what genuine compensation packages, heritage conservation and environmental mitigation will cost, more are being persuaded to stand back. The withdrawal of the British company Balfour Beatty from the Ilisu dam in Turkey late in 2001 was a case in point. A number of large companies – including some oil giants beleaguered by social and environmentalist protest – have declared their intention of putting their ecological house in order. But many activists believe that commitment is only superficial. The corporate green uniform, they say, is only worn to the extent necessary to keep business on track.

In the run-up to Rio, a Business Council on Sustainable Development consisting of 48 industrialists put forward the view that transnational corporations could espouse green concerns without losing competitiveness in national or global markets – so long as there was a 'level playing field' and the economic costs were shared across the world. But their solutions were purely technocratic – 'a caricature of the Rio spirit'.[4] The idea that the recipe of sustainability lies in making resources more productive by exploiting them more efficiently has since been heavily promoted, even by the Club of Rome.[5] Others scoff at the notion that technology can be used to solve the ecological problems created by – technology. Cars are now more fuel-efficient. But fuel efficiency does not solve the problem of exponentially growing traffic.

While overall consumption rises, all efficiency can do is to buy time. Social scientist Wolfgang Sachs points out: 'An ecology of means has to be accompanied by an ecology of ends. The efficiency revolution will remain counterproductive if it is not accompanied by a sufficiency revolution. Nothing is as irrational as running with high speed and with utmost efficiency in the wrong direction.'[6] A sufficiency revolution would mean a cap on growth – especially in the North. At present, neither North nor South would remotely consider an international agreement on limits to growth, which is what in the end 'sustainability' will have to be about. At present, for the most influential players, sustainable development is more about sustaining the current pattern of development than the tolerance capacity of the ecosystem or of human societies.

The run-up to the second Earth Summit in Johannesburg in August 2002 led to a great deal of breast-beating about what has not happened since the first. UN Secretary-General Kofi Annan has admitted that the 'political and conceptual breakthrough achieved at Rio has not proved decisive.' His view that Johannesburg could turn this around will not be universally shared. Almost every environmental indicator had shown deterioration at the global level in the past ten years. Carbon emissions have increased by nine per cent; coral reefs have doubled their deterioration, from ten to 27 per cent; a quarter of the world's fisheries are now over-fished; 11,000 biological species are threatened with extinction.[7] There have been negotiations and treaties on biodiversity, chemical pollution and climate change. But they contain serious flaws, implementation is weak, and the funds the South needs to enforce them have not materialized.

Meanwhile, whatever has not been done to preserve the biosphere for future generations, what has been happening to the sustainability of the resources which support the livelihoods of those living in poverty today?

Life's essentials: food

At the 1974 World Food Conference in Rome, then US Secretary of State Henry Kissinger made a famous pledge that within a decade, 'no man, woman or child will go to bed hungry'. By the time of the 1996 World Food Summit, 800 million lives in the developing world were still dominated by the threat of hunger. A more modest target was set: to reduce this figure by half within two decades. One old-stager from the South was scathing: 'What kind of cosmetic solutions are we going to provide,' thundered Fidel Castro of Cuba, 'so that 20 years from now there will be 400 instead of 800 million starving people? The very modesty of these goals is shameful.'

Modest or not, the UN's Food and Agriculture Organization (FAO) was already acknowledging by 1999 that they would not be met. Why? Because as in 1974, there was no plan for how to do this, nor recognition of the scale of effort needed. Another World Food Summit met in June 2002, to 'review progress towards the goals' and was treated with widespread derision. The impotence of such meetings is graphically illustrated by the coincidence that 12 million people were facing acute hunger and famine in southern Africa even as the delegates arrived.

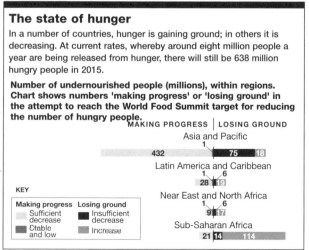

The state of hunger

In a number of countries, hunger is gaining ground; in others it is decreasing. At current rates, whereby around eight million people a year are being released from hunger, there will still be 638 million hungry people in 2015.

Number of undernourished people (millions), within regions. Chart shows numbers 'making progress' or 'losing ground' in the attempt to reach the World Food Summit target for reducing the number of hungry people.

MAKING PROGRESS | LOSING GROUND

Asia and Pacific
432   75   18

Latin America and Caribbean
28   19

Near East and North Africa
9   17

Sub-Saharan Africa
21   14   114

KEY

Making progress | **Losing ground**
Sufficient decrease | Insufficient decrease
Stable and low | Increase

The state of food insecurity in the world 1999, FAO

Hunger, or 'lack of food security' as it is euphemistically known today, is the quintessential indicator of poverty. To have enough to eat, a household either has to have enough land to grow food, or enough cash to buy it – and some reserves for difficult years. According to the World Bank, more than two-thirds of the world's poorest people are rural; in their case, therefore, the essential issue is access to land for cropping or grazing; if they are landless, to work as labor upon it. Income may be supplemented by micro-enterprises based on agricultural products – snack foods, utensils, cloth – that form part of the surrounding economy. This is the kind of economy, with its informal mechanisms, tiny margins and mini-transactions, which few planners even notice, let alone try to bolster.

Unfortunately, no large-scale international effort to promote sustainable rural livelihoods or build food security is based on boosting the economy in which 1,400 million small-scale farming families struggle to survive. Their land is often in marginal areas, where rainfall is inadequate and soils fragile. Ecologically sensitive farming improvements based on traditional drought-resistant crops such as sorghum and millet are what they need. But agricultural policies invariably focus on wheat, rice, export crops – and lucrative markets.

Consolidated smallholdings

The state government of Andhra Pradesh in India recently adopted a policy to modernize agriculture that prides itself on the consolidation of smallholdings and the abandonment of millions of farmers' livelihood systems – in the name of poverty alleviation. Donors, notably the UK, buy into this absurdity. In some Latin American countries, research into small-farmer problems has been abandoned completely; land is not seen as something on which food for people should be grown, but as something from which foreign exchange can be extracted.[8] Where agricultural economists, agribusiness and international crop institutes focus on food, their concern is for harvest size and seed varieties, maximizing yields and land productivity, improving irrigation efficiency and 'crop per drop', not about platefuls of something for the hungry to eat. Their attention is on the big picture.

However, the big picture is no longer looking good. In the past 50 years, world food output nearly tripled – which has bred complacency about hunger and enthusiasm about agribusiness profits. China managed to reduce the proportion of its people suffering from hunger from 30 to 11 per cent between 1980 and 1997, and numbers have also declined in Latin America. But in the world's other very populous and densely settled country, India, and in its neighbors on the South Asian sub-continent, the picture is less good. In India, 53 per cent of children are undernourished and in Bangladesh, the proportion is 56 per cent. Africa gives even greater cause for concern. Here, the balance between people and food has consistently worsened since 1980. In over 20 African countries, including many where the problem was already severe, the proportion of hungry people has risen in recent years.[9]

The expansion of food output cannot be sustained. The efforts of recent decades have imposed major pressures on the environment. New land to plow is scarce. Since 1979, the agricultural land per capita on the planet has diminished by seven per cent, due to fertilizer saturation, desertification caused by woodland loss and salinity caused by bad irrigation. Irrigated farmland nearly doubled between 1960 and 2000 to over 250 million hectares, but 20 per cent of this area has suffered a sufficient build-up of salts in the soil to threaten its eventual fertility.[10] Recently, the costs of opening up new areas to large-scale irrigation combined with poor returns on earlier projects have driven investors away. Farming land has also been lost to the expansion of towns and cities. In all three of the world's food systems – cropland, rangelands and fisheries – the train is beginning to hit the buffers. Since

1990, the rise in the production of animal protein has tailed off, and oceanic fish catches have declined by ten per cent. So future growth in the world's food basket poses a challenge, independently of the other challenge: who gets to eat from it.

Water wars

Prospects are made more complicated by severe stresses on water resources, 70 per cent of which are consumed in agriculture. More than 230 million people live in the 26 countries already designated as water-short, mainly in Africa and the Middle East, and their numbers are growing. There is talk of a global crisis of over-extraction and consumption of water, leading to 'water wars'. By 2025, three billion people will live in countries that have less than 1,700 cubic meters a head, the quantity below which populations start to suffer from water stress.[11]

Cities and industries are already competing with agriculture for scarce supplies, while water tables everywhere are dropping, and rivers and aquifers becoming more polluted. The pressures come not just from population growth, but from water-intensive farming, water-profligate urban life-styles and reckless attitudes towards wastes. Unless water-use trends change radically, it is unclear how long the world's

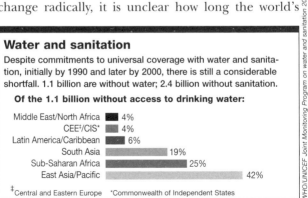

Water and sanitation

Despite commitments to universal coverage with water and sanitation, initially by 1990 and later by 2000, there is still a considerable shortfall. 1.1 billion are without water; 2.4 billion without sanitation.

Of the 1.1 billion without access to drinking water:

Middle East/North Africa	4%
CEE‡/CIS*	4%
Latin America/Caribbean	6%
South Asia	19%
Sub-Saharan Africa	25%
East Asia/Pacific	42%

‡Central and Eastern Europe *Commonwealth of Independent States

WHO/UNICEF Joint Monitoring Program on water and sanitation 2000 finite supply of freshwater and natural self-cleansing properties can cope. Just as there are hundreds of millions of people suffering from food insecurity, there are similar numbers suffering from water insecurity and health-threatening pollution. At last count, 1.1 billion people were without a supply of safe water, and 2.4 billion without proper means of sanitation.[12]

Whenever these matters are internationally discussed, the unsustainability of 'business as usual' regarding patterns of land and water use is endlessly lamented. The numbers of those whose lives are barely sustainable now because of food and water shortages are cited in evidence. But the degree to which 'business as usual' has actually brought about their plight is less well acknowledged. Few really poor people live in lush, irrigated plains. If they do, it is only as the cheapest of labor or in densely settled delta areas such as Bangladesh where holdings are tiny. Over time, most have been squeezed out of productive soils onto arid or semi-arid fringes, or up the slopes of hillsides where erosion is at its worst.

The pressures on such marginal lands quickly denudes them: hunger often goes hand-in-hand with ecosystems reduced to wastelands because there was no other way to grow a crop. Farmers in Vietnam told inquirers: 'We know that cutting down trees will cause water shortages and making charcoal can cause forest fires, but we have no choice. Because we lack food we have to exploit the forest.'[13] Measures introduced to control the loss of woodland further discriminate against those living in highland or wilderness areas. Indigenous people without title to land become excluded, designated 'encroachers' of their own territory.

Putting a price on water

As far as water is concerned, the main tool proposed for its conservation is to put a price upon it that reflects its economic value. Undoubtedly, aquifers are being over-pumped and surface water supplies wastefully squandered. But the notion of making people in traditional rural communities pay for a 'free' natural resource has also provoked outcry – it is not their over-pumping, industrial plants, leaking pipelines, sewerage systems and major irrigation works which are causing the problem. The idea of allowing them a basic right to a small quantity of water – 15 liters a day is one meager suggestion – for drinking and the basic minimum of domestic tasks misses the point. The rural household needs water not just to survive, but to grow food, water livestock, and secure other parts of their livelihood.

Even in water provision, the corporate sector increasingly enters the frame, displacing government and ending the subsidization of services. In the name of efficiency and water savings, the prospects are that they will gain ascendancy over both the resource and delivery systems. In the process they will also destroy traditional systems of water provision and those in the informal economy who depend on these for a livelihood. Thus the hold of poor people on another essential commodity, and on incomes derived from its provision, also looks precarious.

GM – a magic bullet?

Many of the technological and market-oriented solutions proposed to deal with land and water scarcity do, in fact, amount to 'business as usual', only with extras: measures that put tariffs between people and their natural resource base in the name of 'efficiency' and 'management by demand'. The hybrid seeds of Green Revolution fame, and the inputs of fertilizers and pesticides that go with them, are costly to grow and can push small farmers into debt or displacement. To bring about the next food production breakthrough, a further revolution is proposed, courtesy of biotechnology. Claims are made on behalf of genetically-modified (GM) new rice varieties: that they will produce 50 per cent higher yields, mature 30-50 days earlier, be more disease- and drought-resistant, and grow without fertilizer or herbicides. They can even be fixed to contain Vitamin A, which would dramatically improve young children's health. Except that a handful of green vegetables, without the high-tech costs, would do the same.

When the UN Development Program (UNDP) announced in early 2002 that it supported GM technology as a way to help those living in poverty, there was an outcry from the non-governmental community. Vandana Shiva, a distinguished Indian environmentalist, believes that promotion of GM crops is a betrayal of the South, and of the poorest sectors of society and their prospects for food security. Research shows, according to Shiva, that 'farmers triple their incomes by getting off the chemical treadmill and out of the debt trap created by purchase of costly seeds and chemicals.'[14] Others believe that, at best, GM is a familiar sort of magic-bullet distraction – just the type of thing that earned a reputation for irrelevancy in the space-conquest atmosphere of the 1960s. It diverts attention from other technologies and farming practices that also raise productivity. And it overlooks costs and economic misfit.

The truth is that in no case in history has the introduction of this kind of technological innovation favored the poorest in society: on the contrary, it erects barriers between poor people and their resource base. There is too big a gap between the economy in which such people currently operate, and the one in which new seeds, additives and inputs are located. If they accept the package they risk becoming locked into a technology they can neither afford nor control. If they do not, they get driven or priced out. Those who gain most are those in command of the technology, and of wider agricultural commodity markets: agrochemical companies and landowners who can afford to take the risk of jumping onto the bandwagon and sharing in its profits.

To ensure that this will be the way it goes, corporations are now busy taking out patents on seeds they have 'discovered' in the South. Under the 1995 WTO agreement on 'Trade-related Aspects of Intellectual Property Rights' (TRIPS), corporate giants such as Du Pont and

Monsanto have managed to gain scores of patents on strains of maize, rice and other key food crops. These strains, originally the birthright of people who have grown them for generations, are now undergoing transgenetic manipulation to improve their performance. They are then promoted back under license to the countries they came from. Vandana Shiva calls this 'biopiracy' and points out that small farmers who normally plant from stored seed can easily fall victim to dependency on this corporate attempt to lock up the food chain and keep its profits in their hands.

Sustainable living, viewed from the ground

The preservation of the global commons – air, ozone and oceans – requires international action and its standard accompaniments: treaties, regulations, financial incentives and the latest technological inventions. But these are no use for promoting sustainable livelihoods based on natural resources.

This is because every location is different. The complex of factors influencing the resource base – topography, geology, soils, water, plants – and people's multiple interactions with it and with each other over its assets, decide whether livelihoods are sustainable or not. If you start from the perspective of the poorest people, you address their specific circumstances.

Robert Chambers, of Sussex University, a life-long advocate of this approach, sees small-scale, sensitive, locally designed and locally managed interventions as ecological and political safeguards against pillage and degradation by commercial interests and the better off. 'Contrary to popular professional prejudice', he maintains, 'when poor people have secure rights and adequate assets to deal with contingencies, they tend to take a long view, holding on tenaciously to land, protecting trees and seeking to provide for their children. Their time perspective is longer than that of commercial interests concerned with early profits from capital, or of conventional development programs concerned with internal rates of return.'[15] Once again, it has been the non-governmental practitioners with their willingness to spend time and effort exploring existing local systems and traditional technologies who have been in the vanguard of 'sustainable' solutions to the livelihood problems of the poor. They are pioneers, or re-discoverers, of techniques such as micro-dams, inter-cropping systems, moisture-conserving crop management and rainwater harvesting techniques to make life and food production more secure for the 600 million farming people living in the dryland areas which cover a third of the earth's surface.

One example of a successful approach comes from the Yatenga province of Burkina Faso (see box). Similar examples can be quoted from all over the world. Similar in that they are small-scale; rely on adapting indigenous technologies or systems of land-water-use management; and that any outside assistance they receive is flexible and low-cost. In all other ways they are unique.

Ecological and social systems are dynamic, and any intervention, to be successful, needs to be tailor-made. Wherever jewels of sustainable development emerge, as with the stone-lined fields of Yatenga, or soil conservation on the eroded highlands of Nepal, or agro-forestry in Haiti, the development industry

Sustainable living in Yatenga

Increasing human pressure and declining rainfall had destroyed the soil in Yatenga, Burkina Faso, forcing farmers into destitution and migration. Some resorted to a traditional method of containing soil and rainfall by piling stones in lines across eroded fields. Oxfam, which had come to help, initially focused on deforestation and growing trees. But when it became clear that the farmers were much more interested in harvesting water for food production, attention shifted. By introducing a simple method of measuring the land's gentle undulations, it was possible to build stone lines along the contours and make them more efficient. The productiveness of these dyked fields in drought years caused the idea to spread like wildfire. Within a very short space of time, 400 Yatenga villages were applying the technique. ■

instantly calls for 'replicability' and 'scaling up'. But often the idiosyncrasies are themselves the clue.

Localized solutions to the sustainability conundrum that cannot be 'rolled out' like a marketing strategy are often regarded as freakish products of distorted – because socially-driven – investment. However, 'replicability' has turned out to be as elusive in development as the pot of gold at the end of the rainbow and 'scaling up' no easier. The Yatenga approach, for example, cannot work where elevations are pronounced and there is no ready supply of stones. Any community management system of a resource base has to grow organically in response to day-to-day requirements; its success in one setting does not necessarily mean it can be parachuted onto a thousand more.

Most indigenous small-scale land and water management schemes suffer from a lack of public assistance in the form of credit, subsidized loans, extension services and technical support. Yet these are always available on large-scale irrigation programs that have a far worse track record. Until recently, official irrigation statistics for sub-Saharan Africa did not even include land irrigated under traditional methods. When FAO retrospectively corrected its figures to include them, the area rose by 37 per cent.[16]

So there are distortions in policy – that support grand-slam approaches and openings for agribusiness, and neglect local forms of sustainable agriculture. Acknowledgement is made that there is no one route to sustainable development. But the development establishment does not seem to understand the implications of this for policy in institutional terms. It does not back the reforms in land ownership, financing or administration that would open up the prospects of poor communities achieving their own forms of sustainable resource-base management. Perhaps the leaps of understanding, structural inhibitions and obduracy of vested interests are just too daunting.

A fresh start?

Since the concept of sustainability was first invented, much that is valuable for poor communities has been done in its name. But nothing like enough. And much of what has been done is a frantic rearguard action against the continuing invasion of their fragile resource base that 'business as usual' represents. Meanwhile, many poor communities see further threats on their horizons – literally – from floods, droughts and other outcomes of global warming.

Not surprisingly, some of those who heralded the 1992 Rio conference's new era of sustainable development feel deeply disillusioned. Could 'Rio+10' at Johannesburg in August 2002, seen by some as just another gigantic talking shop, yet be the opportunity to make a fresh, more sustainable start that UN Secretary-General Kofi Annan insists?

Some would say that this is a political question, not an environmental one at all. The politics of development is where we go next.

1 *Only One Earth* Barbara Ward and René Dubois, WW Norton, 1972. **2** Most demographic statistics are from *World Population Prospects*, UN Population Division. **3** 'Rich planet, poor planet', Christopher Flavin, in *State of the World 2001,* Worldwatch Institute. **4** Gilbert Rist, *The History of Development,* Zed Books, 1997. **5** *Factor Four, A New Report to the Club of Rome,* Ernst von Weizsacker, Amory B Lovins, L Hunter Lovins, Earthscan, 1997. **6** Quoted in *Green Politics*, edited by Anil Agarwal, Sunita Narain and Anju Sharma, CSE and Earthscan, 1999. **7** *State of the World 2002,* Worldwatch Institute. **8** *Hungry for Trade, How the Poor Pay for Free Trade*, John Madeley, Zed Books, 2000. **9** *The State of Food Insecurity in the World*, FAO, 1999. **10** *The Last Oasis*, Sandra Postel, WW Norton and Worldwatch Institute, 1992. **11** *World Water Vision: Making Water Everybody's Business*, William J Cosgrove and Frank R Rijsberman, World Water Council and Earthscan, 2000. **12** *WHO/UNICEF Joint Monitoring Programme for water and sanitation 2000*. **13** 'Crying out for Change, Study for Attacking Poverty', Deepa Narayan, Robert Chambers, Meera K Shah and Patti Petesch, *World Bank Development Report 2000*. **14** Vandana Shiva, Open letter to Oxfam, and *Water Wars: Privatization, Pollution and Profit*, South End Press, 2002. **15** 'Sustainable rural livelihoods', Robert Chambers, in *The Greening of Aid,* ed Czech Conroy and Miles Litvinoff, Earthscan and IIED, 1988. **16** *The Last Oasis,* Sandra Postel, WW Norton and Worldwatch Institute, 1992.

6 Development is political

The political nature of development has been widely ignored. Yet any transformation in society is inevitably a political process. During the 1980s, people's movements in the South sprang up. Since the end of the Cold War, there has been widespread adoption of political and human-rights vocabulary in international debate and policy prescriptions. While some of this is superficial, at the same time a new politics of active resistance to the standard model has flourished in both South and North.

WHEN THE CRUSADE for development was launched, its context was unequivocally geo-political: this was a grand international project to enable newly independent countries to embrace economic progress and bind them into alliance with the West. Thus aid packages from donor to recipient governments were based on many considerations other than need – especially on the building of strategic and trading partnerships. But the internal dynamics of the mission were not seen as political – rather, as financial and technocratic.

'Development' had little to do with politicians, still less with political scientists; it was a matter for economists, engineers and planners. Where poor people were concerned, as was the case for philanthropic activity, welfarist and humanitarian perceptions ruled, and the task was seen as mopping up politically innocent distress. When social concerns won the right to be viewed as developmental too, the provision of education and healthcare was equally regarded as non-political: these were about building human capital and wellbeing. After this was achieved, a mature and democratic political system would surely materialize. Few considered that poverty reduction would, in itself, be a highly political process.

On their side, the IMF/World Bank and UN bodies

were rigorously bound not to interfere in the internal politics of sovereign member states. So any mission launched under their auspices must be one from which all taint of politics was extruded. What might politically result from any transfer of resources, and whether such transfers could, or should, have a political purpose were subjects beyond the pale. The only political issue the international bodies attended to was the crude one of not taking sides: staying above the divide in any dispute between states or parties within them.

Tackling root causes

While Northern governments used development aid for overtly political and strategic purposes, the more progressive non-governmental players viewed the political context of development very differently. It soon became obvious to them that tackling the root causes of poverty was an inherently political business – which was why they saw development as preferable to pouring money into the bottomless cup of welfare support.

In the early, naive days, the idea of development was encapsulated by a widely repeated proverb: 'Give a man a fish, and you feed him for a day. Teach him to fish, and you feed him for life.' But knowing how to fish often turned out to be the least of his – or her – problems. The river might be polluted and the catch depleted. The trees from which boats were traditionally built had been cut down by loggers, or the right to fish on that waterway granted to others with powerful patrons and larger boats. Fishing families were forced to sell their catch to a marketing board, which depressed producer prices, so that they could no longer make a living. In these situations, the 'knowledge transfer' needed was not how to fish, but the skill to organize, bargain collectively, expose misappropriation and get corrupt officials off their backs.

It became clear that interventions to support livelihoods not only had to fit economic and social realities, but also to contend with power structures. If they did not, vested interests might destroy them or co-opt every benefit to themselves.

Control over resources

Since development requires new configurations in the use and distribution of resources of land, money and human energy, there will be disputes among individuals and groups, which can only be sorted out by a political process.[1] If the existing organization of resources discriminates against the poor, as it invariably does, helping them to make permanent improvements in their circumstances will be problematic. The notion of an expanded cake from which largesse may be neutrally distributed is a fiction. Confrontations – with landowners, party bosses, those with economic or administrative muscle – are bound to occur. It is therefore an illusion to think that the dirty business of politics can be ignored. Nonetheless, it is an illusion to which donors cling, insisting that the sovereign behavior of governments, however unjust and discriminatory towards the disadvantaged, is not an outsider's affair.

Within democratic societies, there are mechanisms for negotiating changes in access to resources. They may not always work well, but at least they are there. In non-democratic societies, or in societies where the hierarchy of power is so entrenched and socially legitimized as to override a democratic veneer, it is extremely difficult for weaker groups to assert their right to a decent share of any cake. Few countries in the developing world enjoy a consolidated democracy, either within their formal political structures or in the rest of their institutions. In Latin America, modern political models were superimposed on pre-modern societies and markets at independence; representative democracy did not grow from organic and socially inclusive processes.[2] The same goes for most of Asia and all of Africa. Governments may be elected, but that does not make society democratic.

Development is political

When development is introduced in circumstances of gross inequality, it too will suffer from gross inequality and in all likelihood will reinforce it.

If there is a program to build power stations, drill boreholes, or construct clinics, politics will play a part in decisions about where they are put, and who owns and runs them. All the way down from the national planning commission, to the district council, the village, even to the household, the exercise of power decides who gains first or most from any improvement. New amenities will not by-pass the homes or communities of the influential on their way to poorer ones unless some countervailing force ensures that this happens.

Inequality data

Except within some specific studies of particular communities or population groups, there is very little data on inequality. Since people who have no power over resources are also excluded from formal political processes, economic exclusion is the best surrogate for political exclusion: there is no data at all on the latter. The UN Development Program (UNDP) and the UN University have recently launched a World Income Inequality Database to improve international analysis of poverty.

Income of poorest 20 per cent of the population 1990-96

In many countries the poorest receive a minuscule share of national income.

	Share of income or consumption (%)	Share as ratio to an equal proportion (%)
Brazil	2.5	13
Chile	3.5	18
Gambia	4.4	22
Indonesia	8.0	40
Jordan	5.9	30
Kyrgyztan	6.7	34
Mexico	3.6	18
Mongolia	7.3	37
Russian Federation	4.2	21
Senegal	3.1	16
South Africa	2.9	15
Thailand	5.6	28
Tunisia	5.9	30
Zimbabwe	4.0	20

When development as economic growth was under critique in the 1970s, people in some parts of the international development industry began to highlight the political dimension – without acknowledging the inherently political nature of what they were suggesting. They called for 'redistribution with growth' and 'growth with equity'. The problem was that, unless a country was politically committed to equitable development – which in the case of China, Cuba and Tanzania was expressed as socialism and therefore an ideological anathema – there was little fertile ground for such ideas. The countries of the Western alliance might deplore the growing number of military dictatorships and one-party states, but the last thing they would do was encourage anything that looked like radical leftist opposition.

The rise of people's movements

While the international establishment kept politically aloof from the growing state of North-South inequity, progressive NGOs in the North complained vociferously about the raw deal poor countries and poor people within them were getting. In the UK, such organizations ran a protracted battle to be allowed to campaign on these issues and were threatened with loss of their charitable status for behaving 'politically'.[3] Their attempts in the field to help poor people exert more control over their lives increasingly confronted the organizations with political dilemmas. These emerged earliest in military-dominated Latin America, especially in north-east Brazil.

Here, poverty's basics – low income, low skills, illiteracy, hunger and ill-health – interacted with violent oppression against indigenous groups in the Amazonian rainforests, dispossession of peasant lands and continuing forms of rural slavery. Recife, its capital, was a crucible of radical thinking on the continent and the hometown of the internationally renowned Archbishop Helder Camera: 'When I give food to the poor, they call me a saint. When I ask why the poor have no food, they call me a communist.'

During the 1970s, under the inspirational leadership of priests, local leaders and disenchanted professionals, a number of grassroots movements emerged on the continent. Many were intent on improving members' agricultural output, literacy and health – an impeccable menu for social development; but they set about this by mobilizing and 'empowering' people to act on their own behalf. Their demand for access to resources was threatening to the iron-clad disciplinarians then in power. The progressive arm of the church became the seat of protest about the condition of those living in poverty, and all the rhetoric and sometimes the armed violence of anti-communism was used against them. As civil war overtook Guatemala, Nicaragua and El Salvador, many local leaders were arrested, and communities that had transformed themselves with some outside help – in the Guatemalan highlands for example – were deliberately massacred. For those caught up in this, the politics of development were unavoidable.

Hard choices had to be made: 'empowerment' could invite state repression. Without empowerment, assistance merely propped up the forces of oppression. In such settings, championing poor people had to mean opposing the state. Many Latin American analysts held that poverty was structural and embedded in the political status quo.

A new form of liberation struggle

During the 1980s, grassroots organizations emerged in many parts of the world. Some of these began as actions to enable poor people to exert control over resources they needed – the Self-Employed Women's Association (SEWA) in Gujarat, India, for example, enabled women trading in the informal sector to avoid dependency on money-lenders and resist police fines.[4] Others mounted resistance to large projects or destructive resource extraction. These included the Chipko movement in the Himalayas which tried to save trees and stop erosion of farming land, and a growing number of movements against dams: one of the largest, in India's Narmada Valley, was launched in 1985.

Another was the rubber-tappers union of Brazil, a collective of associations under their leader Chico Mendes, formed to resist forest clearances that were ruining their livelihoods. Mendes was assassinated in 1988, tragically ensuring that the world knew all about the bitterness of their struggle. The Grameen Bank in Bangladesh was another example; although not overtly political, it asserted the right of the 'unbankable' to enter the credit-entitled world, thereby challenging anti-poor discrimination inherent in many institutions critical to development. By the end of the decade, the rise of social movements in the South – a phenomenon compared to earlier liberation struggles – was attracting considerable attention.[5]

The key feature of these multiplying movements was that they were authentic expressions of people's will and action on their own behalf. All generated their own momentum, avoiding the trap of dependency on external ideas or funds. They wanted to show that they were not some appendage of a Northern-based alternative movement or an offshoot of the development industry; they could control resources, manage activities, develop policies and protest injustice from their own mass base of support. Some were overtly political, mobilized around a particular issue; mostly they did not have a general ideological program. Northern solidarity groups have given support, often providing an advocacy platform to enable them to reach an international audience.

In the 1980s, when the Cold War was still at full blast, the respective political positions of governments and NGOs in both North and South were clear-cut. They were, in a word, adversarial. Donor governments

Cochabamba: political rage over water

In 1999, under World Bank pressure, Bolivia privatized water supplies in water-short Cochabamba city to introduce 'realistic' prices. A monopoly was given to Aguas del Tunari, owned by the US engineering giant Bechtel. The company took over water systems constructed and run by small independent co-operatives without compensation, and introduced charges. People had to buy permits to collect rainwater from their own roof tanks.

Prices shot up, with increases of $20 a month in a region where the minimum wage is under US$100. An organization called the Coordinadora – Co-ordination for the Defense of Water and Life – sprang into being. It was a unique coalition of labor activists, rural organizations, politicians, non-governmental organizations, local professionals and young people. In April 2000, after several months of simmering protests, the citizens took over the city square. Around 80,000 people took to the streets. In retaliation, the Government declared martial law and sent in troops.

As an outcome of the ensuing street battles, Aguas del Tunari packed up and beat a hasty retreat from the country. So far, neither they, nor any equivalent have returned. But the policy they represented, in Bolivia and elsewhere, is still very much alive. ■

William Finnegan, 'Leasing the rain', *The New Yorker*, April 8 2002;
New Internationalist 338, September 2001.

sometimes deplored their allies' inefficiency and increasingly slapped their economic and financial wrists, but they stayed aloof from the regime's internal politics, pleading 'non-interference' as it suited. Whereas the people's organizations stirring in many Southern countries often represented the closest thing to a 'political' opposition practically allowed. They not only expressed dissent with the existing order, but also provided some basis for a developmental and democratic alternative.

Although such organizations had a left-wing ideology, they were not usually aligned with existing political parties. Even in so-called democratic societies, they usually rejected party politics; though they might try to gain allies within them, they believed that conventional political routes to 'right the wrongs' were mediocre, corrupt and could not be depended upon.

When 'people's power' as a political force managed

to topple authoritarian and corrupt regimes – Marcos in the Philippines and Duvalier in Haiti – development could never again be painted as purely economic and neutral. With the end of the Cold War and the triumph of the capitalist and democratic model of society, a different type of political engagement began.

The rise of civil society

The heady days following the collapse of Communism felt like the dawn of a new development era. There was, firstly, the illusion of the 'peace dividend' which would enable aid to flow. More importantly, a tide of freedom was sweeping into the furthest reaches of the world. The struggle for liberty in Eastern Europe, and the demand for development 'for the people and by the people', must surely be two sides of the same coin. The downfall of Pinochet in Chile, of Mobutu in Zaire (now DR Congo), the arrival of majority rule in South Africa, the end to civil conflicts in Central America – all were ushering democracy into places from which it had been long absent. In a world released from the stranglehold of superpower stand-off, tyrants would no longer be supported as bulwarks against the communist foe and democratic forces would surely be allowed to flourish.

The NGOs reveled in their new legitimacy as manifestations of 'civil society' – whose hour, definitively, had come. Their success at mobilizing people behind a localized process of change was treated with adulatory approval, and even the smallest organized expressions were brought within the loop of development policy and practice. 'Civil society' was congratulated for succeeding where bureaucracy had failed, and its role in the new world order was officially welcomed. Alongside the opening up of markets, deregulation and privatization – the whole IMF/World Bank/World Trade Organization (WTO) package – ran an agenda for political reform: calls for democracy and 'good governance'. The triumphant orthodoxy was that open markets, competent administrations

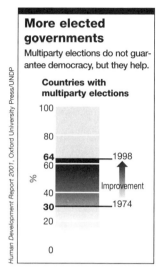

More elected governments

Multiparty elections do not guarantee democracy, but they help.

Countries with multiparty elections

and liberal-democratic politics – the key attributes of Northern capitalist democracies – were alone capable of bringing about development.

In their new capacity, NGOs in both North and South were now partners of governments and accepted in forums where policy was discussed. But the relationship was not easy: there were suspicions on both sides. From governments, there was still an attitude of lofty patronage towards sometimes polemical, sometimes naive, sometimes self-seeking, cuckoos in the nest. On their side, the more vociferous people's movements were unconvinced by the economic agenda and not sure that the political one amounted to anything very much. They also risked loss of independence by their new admittance to the 'development club'. If they took funds from official sources, they were less able to criticize their own governments, donor or recipient, and identify with the new political voice.

The potential for new partnerships between governments and people's organizations in the evolution of alternative, genuinely participatory forms of development was unfulfilled. Where a country's vested interests were under challenge, the forces of civil society were still regarded as awkward or downright counterproductive. Their advocacy of an up-front anti-poverty and environmentalist agenda was disdained. In the official view, the role of NGOs was to help lead civil society down the primrose path of assent to the dominant political and economic order, and conveniently help salve the wounds of those who had fallen off the edge. Movements such as the Zapatistas in Chiapas, Mexico, who in 1994 rose up against laws that ended their indigenous system of landowning, were not regarded as the fiery vanguard of a new development critique, but as political rebels plain and simple.

Participation and empowerment

By the 1990s, the whole international development apparatus had begun to incorporate political vocabulary into their policies for the post-Cold War context. There was a need for 'participation', for decisions to be made 'at the lowest appropriate level'. Development required people's empowerment, and 'democratization' was a pre-condition.

Amartya Sen, the Nobel Laureate economist, was the doyen of this idea, writing of 'development as freedom'. In his view, development required: 'The removal of major sources of unfreedom: poverty as well as tyranny, poor economic opportunities as well as systematic social deprivation, neglect of public facilities as well as intolerance or overactivity of repressive states.'[6] Only where these freedoms were assured was it possible for people to live productively in such a way as to promote their own and wider, social development.

Thus the end of the Cold War meant that the monster of politics was tamed. Ideas that a few years earlier might have conjured alarm were now standard fare. But when it came to the crunch, it was hard to see exactly how the international community would bring on the 'freedoms' and remove the 'unfreedoms' described by Sen, or whether they were just garlanding their stock agenda with trendy vocabulary. They tiptoed round the edge of the real politics of development – control over resources, landowning patterns, marginalization, security and decision-making power.

In fact, 'participation' had captured adherents not because it would rearrange power, but because it had useful management, administrative and cost-recovery characteristics. Everyone knew that many development projects had floundered because people had been left out, and that where they were allowed to join in, much more was achieved with less. The same reasoning was now applied to 'empowerment', 'democratization' and 'decentralization'. These would all make development not only more 'effective and efficient', but also more 'equitable and sustainable'.

But could they be realized on the ground? For that to happen, all the permutations of problems facing people trying to make a living on deteriorating soils, degraded rangelands, depleted rivers and in sprawling shantytowns have to be addressed.

The new rhetoric: governance

That such issues are not addressed is, at heart, a local political issue. Matters are not much improved by a new set of catchwords. Where they are dealt with, it is often by a process of rearguard action against practices of deliberate neglect or exclusion. This rarely happens unless some local organization – people's movement, union, or council – pushes for it. Unless somebody knows how to interact with a particular bureaucracy, gain access to resources and negotiate obstructions, the best policy documents achieve nothing. Many talk about creating an 'enabling environment', but laws and policies decreed from on high often enable very little. Many individuals of amazing courage function in a profoundly disabling environment.

In some instances, the structure of regular programs and the types of inputs – basic health and education services for example – ensure that some benefits reach those on the outer edge of society. But most of the international commitment to the 'enabling environment' and other such concepts has been rhetorical. How can they be meaningfully delivered in highly inequitable societies where power over people and resources is entrenched in the hands of an élite? The answer is by 'good governance'. But this, too, is mostly about standards of efficiency relating to the existing way of doing things, not about serious reallocations of power. Good governance usually involves the existing structures doing things more cost-effectively and accountably, and bowing in the direction of certain social and environmental policy norms. It rarely puts people in control of resources or enables them to influence the structures surrounding them – or if it does, only on a very small scale, and around such issues as garbage removal, not around land tenure or conflict.[7]

In a few contexts – those that do not seem really threatening – there have been successful challenges to existing power structures. One is gender. Women have pointed out that their exclusion from education, training and employment has negative economic effects for a country, and that unless patriarchal power over their lives is reduced, nothing will change. If women are to participate in development, a more equal distribution of political as well as economic power is needed. For a grassroots women's group in Bangladesh for example, 'empowerment' is not just about gaining access to credit or childcare services. It is about defending their rights not to be subjected to violence or abandoned, and this demands sufficient influence on local leaders to induce community sanctions against errant husbands.

On behalf of women, children and to a lesser extent, indigenous groups, there has been some institutional willingness to take up political cudgels. The way this has been done however is less through the language of politics than through the language of human rights.

The ascent of rights

During most of the Cold War, the pursuit of rights at the international level was submerged within the great ideological contest. In addition to the Universal Declaration of Human Rights, a number of human rights treaties were passed by the UN General Assembly, but most accusations of human-rights abuse were seen as a cloak for attacks on the Communist system or other

Human Development Report 2001, Oxford University Press/UNDP

Ratification of human-rights treaties

Countries ratifying the 6 major human rights conventions and covenants

Since the 1948 Universal Declaration of Human Rights, a number of human-rights treaties have been agreed by the UN General Assembly and subsequently passed into international law. Most countries have signed or ratified them. A major exception is the US, which has been unwilling to ratify almost any, including those protecting women, children and economic and social rights.

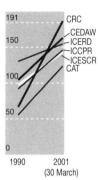

Key:
CRC = Convention on the Rights of the Child
CEDAW = Convention on the Elimination of all forms of Discrimination Against Women
ICERD = International Convention on the Elimination of all forms of Racial Discrimination
ICCPR = International Convention on Civil and Political Rights
ICESCR = International Convention on Economic, Social and Cultural Rights
CAT = Convention Against Torture

non-sympathizers with Northern values.

Human-rights activists mainly focused on deprivations of individual civil and political rights, such as freedom of speech and freedom from arbitrary arrest. Although there were also international conventions on social and economic rights, these were regarded as 'aspirational': freedom from poverty was not a right that could be attained by legislation. The fact that 'justice' could not be present where high proportions of the population had no access to education, a decent diet, or a productive livelihood was unfortunate, but development would have to provide these before universal rights to such things could be meaningfully claimed.

The end of East-West ideological confrontation came at a time when this position was increasingly under challenge. Development was not taking care of these problems, and instead was often precipitating deprivations of 'freedom': conflict, forced migration, child labor. The 'human needs' argument for development had proved too puny. A much broader interpretation of human rights than the old demands for liberty and freedom of expression should now be brought to development's assistance. If that was done, the inequalities reinforced by current development patterns could be challenged, and the rights of the excluded could be upheld with the aid of laws, constitutional provisions and international treaties.

Interestingly, the human-rights instrument that did most to legitimize the new thrust for the fulfillment of social and economic rights was the 1989 UN Convention on the Rights of the Child. This convention, to which every country except the US and Somalia became a party within a few years – a unique human-rights achievement – combined social and economic rights with civil and political ones. The rights of children to survival, a family upbringing, access to health and education, were enshrined in international law, alongside their rights to non-discrimination, freedom from exploitation, and to have their voices heard. Child-related organizations pushed countries to bring their legislation into line with the convention's provisions. No longer were policies concerning children a matter of beneficence. All children had rights which states had sworn to protect and uphold, and this had implications for public spending, law enforcement, criminal justice and so on. Governments had made a political commitment – one few had anticipated, because children are not supposed to be political beings.

Another important step for human rights was taken when the 1993 UN Conference on Human Rights in Vienna affirmed that 'the human rights of women and of the girl child are an inalienable, integral and indivisible part of universal human rights'. This explicit international commitment that forms of abuse or discrimination based on sex or gender – rape, girl infanticide, female genital mutilation, trafficking of girls – were full-scale abuses of human rights was won only after a long struggle.

A shifting framework

These and other rights initiatives were increasingly

seen as a basis for rectifying inequalities and lack of social justice. Instead of depending on the kindness of policy-makers, activists and victim groups began to have recourse to the law in their campaign to get things changed. International organizations felt able to speak out about rights violations without inhibitions about interfering in sovereignty or local cultural practices.

The shift to rights as the framework for development action has been welcomed by people's movements in the South. No longer is the championship of rights left to Amnesty International and a handful of specialist organizations; rights have become a common currency. Recourse to the courts as a remedy for developmental injustice is more common. Advocacy has helped bring out into the open issues which governments prefer to brush under the carpet. Slavery, for example, in its contemporary forms of debt bondage and human trafficking, receives far more attention than a decade ago. Many Southern activists, adept at deploying international networks of support, welcome international outcry over such practices. The rights of indigenous peoples are the basis for protesting their loss of habitat. The right of children not to be sexually exploited is the basis of initiatives against sex tourists. Refugees, internally displaced people, and the ethnically cleansed have made similar recourse to the defense of their rights under international law.

The rights agenda may have the edge over the well-being agenda when it comes to advocacy on behalf of poor people. It has helped many development actors find common political cause. But the capacity of international action to make a difference where it matters is necessarily limited. Many governments routinely flout people's rights while signing up to treaties that demand the opposite. There is no way to bring perpetrators legally to book: admonition is the only weapon of international monitoring committees. No international court could ever be established that could process more than a handful of spectacular cases. International partners in development programs often fail to notice the everyday discrimination and rights evasion occurring under their noses. Where they do notice, they may feel unable to protest, or their protest may be ignored. Governments complain that they do not have the resources to fulfil such rights – for example, that of all their citizens to basic education.

Rights is the latest development discourse, and much of the attention has been theoretical or rhetorical – another avenue for venting frustration. And the debate may soon subside. The rights and democracy agenda seems to be losing ground in a world unnerved by the events of September 2001.

The tide of resistance

In November 1999, 50,000 people gathered in Seattle to disrupt World Trade Organization (WTO) talks on a new round of trade liberalization. Protesters and African delegates outraged by their marginalization caused the collapse of negotiations. This demonstration of people's power, accompanied by teargas and street battles, witnessed the emergence of a new international political movement.

The vast majority of protesters were trying peacefully to influence discussions that they believed had no democratic legitimacy and whose intended outcome would impoverish people and the planet. But reaction and counter-reaction became violent. Every subsequent international meeting of this kind – the G-8 (seven rich world countries plus Russia), World Economic Forum, annual meetings of the World Bank and IMF – has since been threatened by mass protest. Disruptions in Quebec City, Prague and Genoa have led to their location in fortress-like settings.

Signs of resistance had been accumulating. In 1998, Subcomandante Marcos, the leader of the Zapatistas in Mexico said: '[Our movement] is a symptom of something more… When we rose up against the

Government we began to receive displays of solidarity and sympathy not only from Mexicans but from people in Chile, Argentina, Canada, the US and Central America. They told us that the uprising represents something that they wanted to say, and now they have found the words to say it.'[8]

Mass protests in many Asian countries took place in the wake of the financial crisis of 1997, by farmers and small-scale entrepreneurs for whom the crash brought ruin. Other similar uprisings have since occurred in Ecuador, Brazil and Nigeria. In India, a National Alliance of People's Movements with over 100 member organizations resists the onslaught conducted by economic liberalization against people's lands and ways of life.

The new politics, whose loose ideology is the defense of social justice and environmental integrity, lambasts 'globalization' – the integration of the global economy on terms devised by international bankers and corporations with governmental connivance. This common thread connects a patchwork of organizations in North and South and their profusion of local agendas. Their resistance underlines the contradiction at the core of global economic advance: the existing strategy for mass prosperity comes at the cost of creating immediate poverty for millions. Transnational corporations exert increasing economic control over the lives of poor communities, but have no allegiance to the countries in which they live and no empathy with movements operating on their behalf. Even organizations that ought to be in solidarity show an extraordinary detachment. In the words of an official of the UN's Food and Agriculture Organization (FAO), people displaced from their lands are 'variable factors of off-farm production', not families who have lost their livelihoods.[9]

The outcry globalization has evoked shows that the grand 'economic reform' agenda is in fact a political project, eliciting a political response. Those who form part of the new consensus are, in their different ways, rejecting development in its contemporary form. Many see the international politics of resistance as a glorious renaissance in a world de-politicized by the Communist collapse. But the problem is that the movements are anarchic in the political sense of the term: without political leaders, without a manifesto, without a common platform or plan.

In most countries, even in the North but especially in the South, they function outside the existing structure of organized politics – which they deeply distrust. They are stating clearly what they do not want, and illustrating within their own structures a more humane, ecologically sound and democratic way of being. But it is hard to see how they can effect a major transformation of policy and practice either inside countries or globally without assaulting, by an extensive political project of their own, the current citadels of power. And to do that they need to play a part in organized political life and to develop agendas which carry political weight in their settings.

In the new world fearfulness created by the attacks on the US on 11 September 2001, in which dissident views expressed by civil society are viewed with foreboding, that task seems more daunting than ever.

1 *States of Development: On the Primacy of Politics*, Adrian Leftwich, Polity Press, 2000. **2** *NGOs: fragmented dreams*, in *Debating Development*, Jaime Joseph, ed Deborah Eade and Ernst Ligteringen, Oxfam GB, 2001. **3** *A cause for our times,* Maggie Black, Oxford University Press/Oxfam, 1992. **4** *Democratizing Development,* John Clark, Earthscan 1991. **5** *New Social Movements in the South,* ed Ponna Wignaraja, Zed Books, 1993. **6** *Development as Freedom,* Amartya Sen, Oxford University Press, 1999. **7** *Poverty Report 2000*, United Nations Development Program, New York/Oxford, 2000. **8** 'To open a crack in history, faces of global resistance', quoted by Katharine Ainger, *New Internationalist* 338, September 2001. **9** *Hungry for trade,* John Madeley, Zed Books, 2000.

7 Where next?

At the end of trying to work out what 'development' means and whose interests the process serves, it is tempting to echo those who regard the mission as defunct. However, neither the concept nor the activities carried out in its name are likely to vanish. More could be done to re-cast 'development' so that it actually serves those for whom it was always supposed to be intended. More legitimacy for poor people as equal partners in the process, rather than as objects of development, would be a good starting-point.

AT THE OUTSET of this guide, a central dilemma was posed. How could an end-state and a process – 'development' – that was meant to be synonymous with poverty reduction have been subverted in such a way as to reinforce the poverty of millions of people?

The dilemma remains. Too often, the pursuit of development fails to address the contradictions between its expressed purpose and its actual effects. Whatever positive gains some development actions can and do achieve, others drive millions of people into a miserable existence and reduce women and children into marketed objects of servitude. They also banish the voices of poor people from debate over actions that ruin them, violate human rights and inflict intolerable losses on both human and natural systems. Instead of reducing gaps between North and South and between rich and poor within them, development has actually caused them to widen.

Under these circumstances, it is tempting to join the ranks of those who have already announced the demise of the development idea, dismantled its underlying economic theory, or dismissed it as a myth.[1] But attractive as it might be to lay to rest this outmoded and divisive concept, it is hard to know how. Despite five decades of dashed hopes, the development industry is not in retreat: far from it. More studies and analyses of its various dimensions are produced by the day. More people are employed. More research students ponder 'knowledge transfer' and 'participatory appraisal'. For the first time since the early 1990s, resources for development co-operation are on the rise. Since the attacks of September 11 2001, articles about development have become more common, even appearing in *New Yorker* magazine.[2]

Even at the purely semantic level, the term 'development' is very difficult to replace. If you dislike it and its derivatives – 'developing', 'developed' – and try to avoid using them, nothing else quite works. To understand that development was an artificial construct from the start and has earned much discredit does not help to get rid of it. The concept has become ingrained in economic language and philanthropic endeavor. In default of some better terminological alternative, we will probably go on using the one we have. It would be helpful, however, if it was more used with greater care, and not assumed to be invariably beneficent and politically clean.

Over time, the concept of development has expanded. In what we have seen as a loose historical sequence, the original economic parameters have accumulated social and human attributes, respect for the environment, and for democracy and human rights. Perhaps its plasticity has worked to its advantage. Exploring it from these different perspectives hopefully provides a better grasp of its complexity and the tugs of war pulling in different directions. It shows that the quest for answers to the development puzzle cannot be found by advancing on one front without addressing others: they are all inextricably linked. Instead of becoming more clear-cut, this sometimes seems to mire the quest in conflicting and overlapping layers. But then 'development' has always suffered from oversimplification both of problem and prescription.

It should be a cause for celebration, not despair, that there are no clear-cut answers to the conundrum of development. A multiplicity of efforts on many fronts is more likely to reduce more poverty and exploitation than any big-bang theory or new set of global resolutions.

Living with the development puzzle

If we have to live with 'development', then should we redefine what it means? The problem with most definitions is that they tend to describe an idealized state of being, and give little clue as to how a society will arrive at this nirvana. One example was set out in 1990 by the South Commission. This international body was set up in 1987 under the chairmanship of President Julius Nyerere of Tanzania to produce an authentically Southern perspective on what development ought to be about. But the outcome they produced did not resolve its many inconsistencies, or suggest radical new directions that would better serve the poor. If such a Commission with all its panels of experts and work in various continents could not manage this over a three-year period, then one has to wonder whether anyone could.

A continuing problem is that the use of the term is still largely confined to the economic context. This

---

Development according to the South Commission

'Development is a process which enables human beings to realize their potential, build self-confidence, and lead lives of dignity and fulfillment. It is a process, which frees people from the fear of want and exploitation. It is a movement away from political, economic or social oppression. Through development, political independence acquires its true significance. And it is a process of growth; a movement essentially springing from within the society that is developing... The base for a nation's development must be its own resources... Development has therefore to be an effort of, by, and for the people. True development has to be people-centered.' ∎

The Challenge to the South, Report of the South Commission, OUP, 1990.

tends to narrow its meaning to macro-economic performance, conveniently eliding over what is really happening to disadvantaged people. It reinforces the impression that the standard World Bank/IMF development paradigm is the only one around.

Even economically, this paradigm is suspect, since it ignores traditional economies, seeing them as fit for elimination, rather than as adaptive bases for their dependents' present and future livelihoods. This restricted outlook skews the whole picture of what development is or could be about. The macro-economic version needs to be persistently challenged, as does the hypocrisy that, with a little adjustment, a relentless expansion of growth will ultimately serve the poor. Evidence does not support the thesis, and poor people themselves roundly dispute it.

At the opposite end of the spectrum, the humanitarian view of development as a longer-term version of relief, a lasting way of improving the lives of victims of war, disaster, illness or exploitation also has its limitations. This version of development, which has been conveyed to the donor public by NGOs, neglects its social, economic and political contexts. Without regard for context, humanitarian aid creates dependency on structures not integral to the recipient society. Many wrongly assume that humanitarian and developmental dynamics are polar opposites. But all aid should support an organic process of development, not provide an artificial substitute.

In the South, people have to live with the term. They experience 'development' on a daily basis in the form of laws, policies, services, projects, administrative arrangements, and employment and entrepreneurial opportunities. 'Development' goes on all about them in one form or another, even intruding into remote environments people once thought of as uniquely theirs. For them, development in its current form is something to resist. What they want is not an end to it, but an end to the damage being done in its name, for which a different, better contextualized, more authentic model might prove the antidote.

Much has been done in the past decade to rebrand the term by emphasizing human values and the pursuit of democracy and human rights. This attempt to refocus on people has helped re-direct some hearts and minds in the donor community, and exerted some influence on policies and official attitudes in the South. However, the synthesis of human development into something defined by progress towards certain measurable goals begs many questions. It does not capture many predicaments of exclusion, family breakdown, child or female exploitation, nor the collapse of traditional protective networks or the ongoing destruction of once viable ways of life. Instead, we end up with another macro-analysis.

However often it is repeated that there are no universal prescriptions for development, the annual international analyses and 'agendas for action' suggest the opposite. They support the gravitational pull of the idea that the macro level is where development is at. In this scenario, the third-to-half of humanity living in poverty are merely an unfortunate corollary to the positive story of socio-economic progress.

Putting poor people first

The development process advocated by this *Guide* would be one that helped bring about an empathetic transition from a traditional way of life to one in which choice and opportunity are expanded and health and productivity improved. In this vision, communities themselves would manage the process of engagement with the benefits offered by scientific advance, and their rights in this context would be protected by the state.

This view of development starts from where people, including the most disadvantaged, already are. Improvements in their lives will derive from, or be based on, their existing economic and social realities. The identification of development objectives, and the means of getting there, are tasks for communities and larger collectives to undertake on their own behalf. They cannot be established from outside.

The task of state-level players is to construct a workable administrative and legal framework within which this can be done, trying to ensure that the process of analyzing needs and matching them to practicable strategies for change is undertaken in a democratic way. Politicians and bureaucrats should see that the provision of resources to implement such plans is equitable and properly carried out. This requires them to oppose the social attitudes and behaviors that reinforce discrimination against poor people.

This view of development respects the fact that local idiosyncrasies make or break its prospects in any given setting. If there is economic, technological or managerial misfit; if local people can see that some intended improvement involves them in too much risk; if it is not adapted to the local circumstance; if it can be used by landowners, contractors or officials to exploit local people even more than happens already; if a long list of diverse dynamics are not in favor, the best laid plans will fail.

Much more investment should therefore be put into micro-development planning and its implementation at local level, and in building bridges between informal and traditional economies and the modern domestic economy. Exports to earn foreign exchange may also be necessary, but they should not be the paramount concern. If that means countries cannot pay their debts, then debts should be adjusted or written off. The whole aid and development industry should redesign its machinery to respect that what happens in the local context is central, rather than ornamental, to the great national plan.

Since in many developing societies, poor communities have so few practical means of bringing those in immediate power over them to book, it is essential to enlist organized expressions of their will in the development process. These include all organizations in which they have trust – community groups, NGOs, people's movements, committees, councils and associations. Where these don't yet exist, they need to be nurtured into existence.

Few existing political systems in developing countries have sufficient democratic credentials to champion a more just and effective form of development. Without the leadership of bodies with some claim to authentic popular representation, a process of organic, inclusive and socially cohesive development cannot be achieved. The process of challenging existing structures and insisting on the rights of everyone to resources and opportunities has to be led from, and in the end can only be accomplished in, the South. But it would be to their immense advantage if the international development industry understood and supported this process, instead of getting in the way.

The international circus

This vision of development accords a new role to the 'international community'. At present too much importance is attached to the role of international organizations as instruments of the process.

Too many donors – including Northern NGOs – prop up the notion that there is such a thing as 'international' development. Certainly there is an international development industry, but that is not the same thing. The international apparatus is vital for regulation of the global commons. It is also important as the source of aid. But its role in designing and implementing development is less easy to determine. And too little effort has gone into working it out.

The proliferating international circus – the conferences, summits, commissions, and their magisterial inquiries into the state of the world's this or that – too often imply that, if only the world can reach consensus around key policy principles, the obstacles to develop ment will crumble. Their syntheses of comparative data, the distillation of 'best practice' into thumbnail accounts, convey an impression of progress or its imminent prospect against difficult odds. They have a tendency to describe what needs to be done about forests, nutrition, child prostitution, dams, mining, or public health as if its articulation could bring about a *fait accompli*. But nothing actually happens internationally to redress poverty and injustice for people. Perhaps the idea that it does is an unfortunate mirror-image of its opposite. For undoubtedly, things do happen in international boardrooms and the decision-making bodies of the donor world, which dramatically affect poor people – for the worse.

Why is there no symmetry in this equation? Obviously, the framework of national policy and administration greatly affects the nature and path of a country's development, and international prescriptions can exert an influence on that. But what matters far more is whether and how policies are actually put into effect. Many Southern delegates agree to policy principles stipulated at the international level in order to open wide the donor checkbook. At the same time, they know that circumstances on the ground – social resistance, lack of capacity, refusal by vested interests, costs – mean that they will not be carried out.

Some of the policy principles agreed to – safeguarding the environment, defending human rights, enabling people's participation – are exemplary on paper. But there is often little prospect of their implementation. Their elaboration is so far removed from the experiences of people at the end of the line that it often seems as though local and 'international' development are on different planets.

When you have witnessed the bulldozing of hundreds of shantytown dwellings, or visited homes where family upon family recounts the loss of land, livelihood and family pride to make way for 'development', it is impossible not to feel distaste at international policy-makers' latter-day discovery of truths such as: 'We need to lay more emphasis on managing vulnerability and encouraging participation to ensure inclusive growth.'[3] The very organizations that reduce key ideas to platitudes also make the loans and help create the 'enabling' environment in which pauperization occurs. They are able to claim ignorance because they rely for feedback on specious government reports and have remarkably little genuine understanding of the realities of ordinary people's lives.

The international industry should behave with more realism about its own development role, and become more responsive and accountable to the local setting. Less effort should be put into grand international initiatives – 'Marshall Plans for Africa' and declarations on sustainable development – and more into making things work on the ground.

In the name of 'the poor'

Since the whole rationale for the development mission is to reduce poverty, it seems legitimate to suggest that more of what is done in the name of 'the poor' should actually be designed to serve them. If between a quarter and a third of the people on earth have been failed or by-passed by development, ways have to be found to re-direct the process in their favor.

One way to do this would be to push much harder for the basic services agenda, both within aid programs, and as part of the leverage which external support agencies exert on developing country policies. This implies not only an increase in volumes and in proportions to the 20 per cent or higher already established as a donor-government target, but reforms in the way such services are run. To some extent, this is already happening. But it is not happening enough. The UN millennium targets have given this agenda a boost. But the poverty-reduction strategies put in place as part of IMF/World Bank programs of adjustment need to reinforce the process, not propose privatization and charges for every basic service in sight. At present, many representatives of civil society regard the introduction of these strategies as a public relations exercise to dress up the familiar macro-economic agenda with poverty reduction gloss.[4]

The other key to a radical redirection of development efforts is to confer more legitimacy to poor people's existing strategies. Marginalized people are not passive victims. Their success at coping in the face of almost insuperable odds is evidence of resourcefulness. The vast majority live in an informal, and in some cases invisible, economy that needs to be supported, not eclipsed. Destroying that economy in the name of poverty reduction is the worst form of development hypocrisy. When such things occur, it is understandable that they become equally resourceful at expressing obstruction and dissent. When the power of their resentment is co-opted by agents of ethnic or religious hatred, the consequences – in Afghanistan, Burundi, Rwanda, the Balkans, Kashmir, Gujarat, Palestine and countless other places – can be devastating, to the point of threatening world stability.

Opposing the one-thought world

In the course of the last 20 years, as the crisis of deteriorating terms of existence has descended around them, some Southern movements and associations and the wider networks of organizations which have developed in solidarity with them, have dared to suggest alternatives to the 'one-thought world'.

These are the people in the 21st century who are doing the most to re-shape the development mission. They are not trying to offer a fully articulated alternative vision to capitalism – an ideological new 'big idea'. They are articulating many visions of development, redefining and redesigning its local parameters according to its subjects' needs and capacities. And they are trying to create political space in neighborhoods, communities and at the national and international level, to enable these approaches to flourish.

It is easy to dismiss their efforts as a romantic David versus Goliath competition they are doomed to lose. But the sum of their attempts is the major cause for optimism in the fight to re-inject morality into the development mission. If you go and talk to such people, you will find them reaching out for solidarity, resolute in their determination to defend their rights. 'We will drown, but we will not move,' say people confronted by inundation of their land in India's Narmada Valley. It is part of the human condition that some people, despite all odds, are courageously prepared to take on forces that to most of us seem unstoppable and monolithic. Their struggle to make the world a better and a fairer place is infinitely worthwhile.

1 See for example *The History of Development,* Gilbert Rist, *The Rise and Fall of Development Theory,* Colin Leys, *The Myth of Development*; Oswaldo de Rivero, 'Development: A guide to the ruins', Wolfgang Sachs *New Internationalist*, 232, June 1992, all previously quoted. **2** 'Helping Hands', John Cassidy, *New Yorker,* 27 March 2002; and 'Leasing the Rain', William Finnegan, *New Yorker*, 8 April 2002. **3** *Attacking Poverty*, World Development Report 2000, World Bank. **4** Press release from The Development Group for Alternative Policies and the International Rivers Network: 'Critics' attempts at constructive dialogue find World Bank less than engaging', November 2001.

CONTACTS

International

Focus on the Global South
CUSRI, Chulalongkom University,
Bangkok 10330, Thailand.
Tel: +66 2 218 7363/4/5.
Fax: +66 2 255 9976.
Website: www.focusweb.org

**International Network on
Displacement and Resettlement**
Website: www.displacement.net

One World International
Website: www.oneworld.net

Third World Network
228 McAlister Road,
Penang 10400, Malaysia.
Tel: +60 4 226 6728.
Fax: +60 4 226 4505.
Website: www.twnside.org

World Forum for Alternatives
Website: www.forum-alternatives.net

**Wuppertal Institute for Climate,
Environment and Energy**
PO Box 10 04 80,
42204 Wuppertal, Germany.
Tel: +49 202 2492-0.
Fax: +49 202 2492-108.
Email: info@wupperinst.org
Website: www.wupperinst.org

Aotearoa/New Zealand

Jubilee 2000/Debt Action Network
C/o CWS, PO Box 22-652,
Christchurch.
Tel: +64 3 366 9274.
Fax: +64 3 365 2919.

Australia

Australian Council for Overseas Aid
14 Napier Close, Deakin, ACT 2600.
Tel: +61 (2) 6285 1816.
Fax: + 61 (2) 6285 1720.
Website: www.acfoa.asn.au

Canada

Alternatives
3720 Parc Ave, #300,
Montreal, Quebec H2X 2J1.
Tel: +1 514 982-6606.
Fax: +1 514 982-6122.
Email: alternatives@alternatives.ca
Website: www.alternatives.ca

North-South Institute
55 Murray Street, Suite 200,
Ottawa, Ontario, Canada K1N 5M3.
Tel: +1 613 241-3535.
Fax: +1 613 241-7435.
Website: www.nsi-ins.ca

**Canadian Center for Policy
Alternatives**
#410-75 Albert Street,
Ottawa, ON K1P 5E7.
Tel: +1 613 563 1341.
Fax: +1 613 233 1458.
Website: www.policyalternatives.ca

UK

**International Institute for
Environment and Development**
3 Endsleigh Street,
London WC1H 0DD.
Tel: +44 20 7388-2117.
Fax: +44 20 7388-2826.
Email: mailbox@iied.org.
Website: www.iied.org

Jubilee Research
New Economics Foundation,
Cinnamon House, 6-8 Cole St.,
London SE1 4YH.
Tel: +44 20 7089 2853.
Fax +44 20 7407 6473.
Website: www.jubileeplus.org

World Development Movement
25 Beehive Place,
London SW9 7QR.
Tel: +44 20 7737 6215.
Fax: +44 20 7274 8232.
Email: wdm@wdm.org.uk
Website: www.wdm.uk.org

US

D-Gap
927 Fifteenth Street, NW - 4th Floor,
Three McPherson Square,
Washington DC 20005.
Tel: +1 202 898-1566.
Fax: +1 202 898-1612.
Email: dgap@developmentgap.org
Website: www.developmentgap.org

**Institute for Food and
Development Policy (Food First)**
398 60th St, Oakland, CA 94618.
Tel: +1 510 654 4400.
Fax: +1 510 654 4551.
Website: www.foodfirst.org

International Rivers Network
1847 Berkeley Way, Berkeley,
CA 94703.
Tel: +1 510 848 1155.
Fax: +1 510 848 1008.
Email: info@irn.org
Website: www.irn.org

Worldwatch Institute
1776 Massachusetts Ave, NW,
Washington, DC 20036-1904.
Tel: +1 202 452-1999.
Fax: +1 202 296-7365.
Email: worldwatch@worldwatch.org
Website: www.worldwatch.org

Bibliography

see notes at the end of each chapter

Internet Resources
Department for International Development, UK: www.dfid.govt.uk
Center for Science and Environment, New Delhi: www.cseindia.org
Earthscan: www.earthscan.co.uk
Overseas Development Institute, London: www.odi.uk.org
Research Foundation for Science, Technology and Ecology, India: www.vshiva.net
Narmada Bachao Andolan: www.narmada.org
New Internationalist: www.newint.org
Oxfam: www.oxfam.org
United Nations: www.un.org
The World Bank Group: www.worldbank.org

Index

Index